# Good Writing

# Good Writing

## A Composition Program for the Secondary School

Paul Kalkstein

A FEARON TEACHER-AID BOOK
Fearon Teacher Aids, a division of
**Pitman Learning, Inc.**
Belmont, California

**Editorial director:** Roberta Suid
**Editor:** Buff Bradley
**Production editor:** Mary McClellan
**Design manager:** Eleanor Mennick
**Text and cover designer:** J. Terence McGrath

Copyright © 1982 by Pitman Learning, Inc., 6 Davis Drive, Belmont, California 94002. Member of the Pitman Group. No part of this book may be reproduced by any means, transmitted, or translated into machine language without written permission from the publisher.

ISBN-0-8224-3505-5

Library of Congress Catalog Card Number: 81-85353

Printed in the United States of America

1.9 8 7 6 5 4 3 2 1

# CONTENTS

Introduction  1

## PART ONE
## Good Writing—What It Is, How to Teach It

Three Student Compositions—A Critical Look  **4**
Clear and Economical Communication  **6**
Competency Skills  **10**
The Elements of Good Writing  **11**
Developing a Teaching Strategy  **30**
Planning  **31**
Spontaneity  **32**
Flexibility  **32**
Making Assignments  **33**
Helping Students Plan  **37**
Editing and Revision  **39**

## PART TWO
## A Writing Program

Introduction to the Program  **44**
Unit One—Combining Sentences  **48**
Unit Two—Building Paragraphs  **59**

Unit Three—Illustrating a Scene  **64**
Unit Four—Narrating a Journey  **69**
Unit Five—Setting a Mood  **76**
Unit Six—Slanting a Portrait  **81**
Unit Seven—Describing a Process  **86**
Unit Eight—Defining Words and Ideas  **90**
Unit Nine—Comparing Objects and Concepts  **97**
Unit Ten—Analyzing a TV Show and a Book  **105**
Unit Eleven—Analyzing Writing Styles  **114**
Unit Twelve—Arguing a Position  **120**

**Acknowledgments**

Appreciation is extended to the following publishers for permission to reprint material in this book:

Excerpt from page 296 in "Questionnaire" from *One Man's Meat* by E. B. White, copyright © 1942 by E. B. White. Reprinted by permission of Harper & Row, Publishers, Inc.

From page 47 in *Artillery of the Press* by James Reston. Copyright © 1966, 1967 by Council on Foreign Relations, Inc. Published for Council on Foreign Relations by Harper & Row, Publishers, Inc.

Excerpt from page 228 *An American Life* by Jeb Stuart Magruder. Copyright © 1974 by Jeb Stuart Magruder. Published by Atheneum Publishers.

From *Linda Goodman's Sun Signs*, Linda Goodman (Taplinger Publishing Co., Inc., 1968) © 1968 by Linda Goodman. Reprinted by permission.

Thanks also to my students who have given me permission to include their work. Their names appear with their compositions.

# INTRODUCTION

*Good Writing* is based on two premises. The first is that, no matter where we find it, good writing stands out; as teachers of writing we can learn to identify it readily. We can identify it not only because we intuitively sense its quality but also because it exhibits certain specific characteristics. Although the prose of one good writer may differ in scores of ways from that of another, common elements unite them.

The second premise is that once we have identified these characteristics or elements, we can help students to understand them and to employ them in their own writing.

The function of this book is to develop from these premises both a theory of what constitutes good writing and a practical means of teaching students to write well. To this end the book is divided into two parts.

The first half of Part One is an exploration of the elements of good writing. From the general assertion that good writing is "clear and economical communication" follows a list of the elements present in successful writing. These elements, such as *diction*, *emphasis*, and *unity*, are explained at some length. The explanations are intended as background resources for the teacher; they can be used in any writing course, although they are designed for use with the writing program in this book. The discussion of each element ends with Questions for Students. You may type out these questions and give them to students along with a writing assignment, give them selectively to students who are having particular difficulties, or present them aloud when discussing the writing assignments.

The second half of Part One has two aims. First, it outlines the need to remain flexible in teaching writing since students learn in different ways and at different paces. Second, it proposes specific classroom strategies for making assignments, for leading helpful prewriting activities, and for teaching students to edit their papers effectively.

Part Two of *Good Writing* is a writing program of 12 units. The units include a wide variety of writing activities, from sentence combining to writing an argumentative research paper. Each unit is explained, part by part; and each unit is designed to emphasize several of the elements of good writing discussed in Part One. Although discussion of those elements is built into the writing units, it is helpful to refer to Part One for additional detail and further examples while teaching the material in the writing units.

While I hope that *Good Writing* will provide a successful approach to the teaching of writing, I do not expect that this kind of teaching will ever be easy. It requires time, effort, and patience— and more time, effort, and patience. In order to make this expense of energy efficient and helpful, we should first attempt to ascertain the dimensions of the task of teaching writing. So, before examining a basic principle that defines good writing, and before developing the specific elements that characterize good writing, let's step into the classroom and have a look at the complexity of the writing teacher's job.

# PART ONE

## Good Writing— What It Is and How to Teach It

## Three Student Compositions—A Critical Look

Here are three paragraphs from compositions written in class by eleventh graders on the topic "Television Erodes the Imagination" (agree or disagree).

A  T.V. is N.G. By that I mean that if you watch alot of t.v. it will do you no good. You may learn things from t.v. shows, sure, but you never have to think. Take Laverne and Shirly. This show is very funny. Why? Because the audience know what the punch lines will be and starts laughing before they even hear them, its all so obvious they don't even have to think. And on some of these shows they spend so much money on the scenes its all there true to life and you couldn't imagine anything even if you tried.

B  *The process of television watching is, by its very nature, sedentary. The person who watches television is in a trance-like position for hour after hour. As the person watches the set, his or her mind turns gradually into jelly-like substance. The person never uses his or her mental faculties; all he or she does is to receive impressions from the "idiot-box." No imagination is necessary.*

C  *The harder you watch T.V., the more you use your imagination. Although the housewife who uses the set for company while she irons and the tired businessman who listens with half an ear to the news while he sips his drink may not be using their minds, the teenager watching "Happy Days" is busy imagining. He is totally involved with the show, reacting to jokes (this may be passive) and trying to guess what will happen next. After a half hour, he has built up a thousand different imaginary situations based on the one show, and he will continue to imagine what might have happened long after the show is over.*

**Evaluating Them.**  Can we rank these three paragraphs? Of course. Paragraph A is full of errors (spelling, agreement, punctuation) and circular statement. It fails. Paragraph B has no content or originality, although it is free of obvious errors. It passes. Paragraph C is awkward at times, but it is vigorous and original. It gets the best grade. Easy.

But let's not look at the three paragraphs simply from the point of view of a *grader*. The teacher of writing, who must deal with the *writers* of the three papers rather than just with the papers themselves, sees things differently.

As a teacher of writing, you will not have to spend much time with the writer of C. This selection shows a nice balance between generalization and supporting details. Sentence variety is good; so is emphasis. You might suggest that pronouns must be consistent and that a phrase or two would benefit from rewriting (such as the parenthetical comment). But you would bless this writer and send her on her ever-improving way. She probably likes to write and is bending her imagination to the exercise.

You will be spending more time with the writers of A and B. While you would be perfectly correct to flunk A, paragraph B may actually indicate a weaker writer.

Writer B may be glib. How long did it take to write that paragraph? How long for the whole composition? Probably not long at all. Writer B deals in clichés. He may recognize some of these clichés as he writes them (although quotation marks do not make them less trite), but he probably does not realize that *all* of what he has written is cliché: ideas and phrases that go from ether to paper without being filtered through the mind's discriminator.

Writer B is a lazy thinker. He has very likely not even thought about the assigned topic and has merely chosen the position he believes is more fashionable or more acceptable to his chosen audience (his teacher). And then he has just restated that position a number of times without developing it. Nor has he thought kindly of his reader. Many of his phrases are circumlocutions which could be made clearer by shortening: "Process of television watching" to "watching television"; "uses his mental faculties" to "thinks." His verbs are inappropriate—the lazy thinker hates to search for a vivid verb or a precise adjective.

Writer B's sort of writing, which uses many words, often fancy ones, to say nothing, and which never ventures from the general to the specific, is very hard to deal with. This student probably thinks he is a good writer, not a poor one, and will resist efforts to help. He may even have been encouraged by a former teacher to use ornate vocabulary, or semicolons, or compound phrases—without knowing why or when to use them.

Most of all, writer B may be hard to help because this ailment cannot be cured by drill or a handbook. Superficiality must yield to hard work and thoughtlessness to honesty. While guidelines such as those found in books on writing may help, only constant probing of generalities and deflation of puffed-up diction will effectively put such a student on the road to good writing.

The writer of A has, for the present at least, more to build on than B has. She has honesty and interest. There is some vigor in her style, as well as some originality—not all of which results from errors. She apparently has a notion of organization: her paragraph moves from an interesting, if cryptic, topic sentence to a development by example.

We help a writer like A by praising her strengths and by working gradually to eliminate her weaknesses. Spelling and punctuation mastery come with effort and practice; as she writes more and more, she will gain a firmer sense of syntax.

But we must preserve what is valuable in paragraph A—its freshness of style and honesty of approach. We must encourage this writer. She may become a good one, and sooner than we might think.

## Clear and Economical Communication

How is it that we can think of example A as potentially (and I emphasize *potentially*) good writing, while we classify B as mediocre though competent? We can make such judgments by testing a piece of writing against a touchstone, a basic principle that holds for writing wherever we find it: on a billboard or a record album cover, in a newspaper or a State of the Union address—or in a student composition.

This principle is simply stated: *Good writing is clear and economical communication.* Let's analyze the parts of this principle.

***Clear.*** Clear writing is accurate, precise, and free of any unintended ambiguity. It is coherent, clean in syntax, and easy to follow. The core meaning of a sentence, paragraph, or longer piece is emphasized, not hidden. Clear writing is concrete, and it is organized to aid the reader in understanding what the writer has to say. To illustrate:

> Question: *"What can I use to cut this pattern out of plywood?"*
> Vague response: *"You can use that thing over there on that board."*
> Clear response: *"You can use the keyhole saw hanging below the screwdrivers on the tool board."*

The opposite of clear writing is gobbledygook. Unfortunately, students like the writer of paragraph B may be influenced by an alarming number of published models. In an address to a symposium on writing at Texas University at Arlington, Jacques Barzun quoted a sentence in a memo issued by the U.S. Department of Transportation:

> *This is to advise you in accordance with our external audit policy that we do not have requests for the audit of final vouchers for*

> which the audit report will not be issued within six months of the date of your request.[1]

Try that several times. The writer of that sentence lacks the power to think in words and sentences; the prose shows no concern for the audience.

Another kind of writing that often lacks clarity is jargon, words that have meaning for a specific group but that do not communicate well to a general audience. This sentence, written by a school principal to parents, is loaded with jargon; the meaning is all but lost:

> Our school's cross-graded, multiethnic, individualized learning program is designed to enhance the concept of an open-ended learning program with emphasis on a continuum of multiethnic, academically enriched learning using the identified intellectually gifted child as the agent or director of his own learning.

Clear writing demands clear thinking, and it demands thinking in words. Clarity is not simply an intuition or a gift, although some achieve it more easily than others. It may be taught. Teachers who insist on precision of statement and demand rewrites of work that is muddled or ineptly phrased help their students achieve clarity of expression.

**Economical.** Economical writing employs just enough *clear, precise* words to say what is meant, and not one word more. Economical writing avoids circumlocution, euphemisms, and clichés. The economical writer does not produce a string of multisyllabic vocabulary-list words to dazzle the reader; he or she prefers a short word derived from Anglo-Saxon to a long Latinate one.

> Question: *"Why are we decreasing foreign aid to Country X?"*
> Wasteful response: *"Objective examination of our budgetary situation at this time suggests a reprioritizing of our affairs that actually necessitates this cutback."*
> Economical response: *"We don't have enough money."*

Here is an example of uneconomical writing from a book about the Watergate break-in:

> The ad that eventually appeared in the **New York Times** on May 17 was headlined "The People vs. the **New York Times**" and challenged a **Times** editorial assertion that the Vietnam action was "counter to the will and conscience of a large segment of the American people." The full-page ad declared that various polls showed from 59 percent to 76 percent of the people supported the President.

> *I regarded it as an ad that didn't do us much harm but didn't do much good either. It presumably was good for Colson's ego, and perhaps for the President's, as a way of getting back at the* Times, *but to pay the* Times *$4,400 for an advertisement is an expensive way of getting back at them.*[2]
>
> —JEB STUART MAGRUDER

Although the meaning of this paragraph is relatively clear, the paragraph is not economical; what the writer has to say could be said in half the words.

Contrast that paragraph to another one on a political subject. The following paragraph on the power of the president shows how words can be made to do a big job in a limited space:

> *Almost all scientific and political trends are enhancing the power of the President more than they are increasing the power of the Congress or the press. He, alone, has the authority, as Commander in Chief, to order the use of atomic weapons. He is charged with the security of the nation, which rests in large measure on his ability to persuade any hostile power that it cannot make a successful attack on America or America's major allies without risking self-destruction. This assurance rests on a single fact: aircraft and submarines equipped with hydrogen weapons are on patrol twenty-four hours a day in the air and under the personal command of the President. No sovereign in history ever had such power or responsibility.*[3]
>
> —JAMES RESTON

Ornateness hinders economy. Too many writers use elaborate words where simple ones would do—and, in fact, would come closer to the meaning intended. Too many writers pepper their prose with phrases that serve no purpose. Sometimes these are attempts at metaphorical expression; often they are merely clichés. Notice the density of words and poverty of ideas in this partial portrait of a woman born under the astrological sign of Virgo:

> *She has no illusions, so don't try to sell her any phony ideas. To her, truth is beauty—and beauty is truth. Get used to her emptying the ashtrays every three seconds, be kind to her stray kittens, and she'll perform the pipe and slippers routine with feminine grace. She'll share herself cautiously, only with one she trusts, and little things mean a lot to her. Despite her modesty and natural shyness, she's tough enough and strong enough for others to find comforting when dark clouds gather. The quiet courage and deep sense of responsibility of Virgo women often act as a magic glue to hold large families together. She'll probably be a good cook, and she'll never poison you*

with her soup. Your house will be clean and cozy and the big bowl on the coffee table will hold apples instead of chocolate candies (bad for the teeth and general health).[4]

—LINDA GOODMAN

The principle of economy does not rule out interesting or colorful language, of course. Metaphor from a sensitive pen can be a fine and economical means of communication. Here, in a vigorous paragraph, which is economical as well as entertaining, E. B. White discusses the small city:

*There are unmistakable signs which always betray embryonic cities and show that they have the makings of concentration. The presence of pigeons and of English sparrows, those unfailing followers of the smart metropolitan whirl, is a sign. An English sparrow wouldn't be found dead in the country, and it seems to me pigeons feel about the same way; but the minute you get into Main Street there they are, enjoying the hot pavements and the excitement and the congenial vices of congestion and trade. The faces you see on the streets have a slightly different look, too. They are not the faces you left back in the country. You see a fellow and he has a look in his eye, or perhaps it is the way he holds a toothpick in his mouth, as though he knew a secret. And as you pass along in front of the shops you hear the muffled sound of distant bowling balls, the tell-tale thunder of civilization.*[5]

At its best, good writing—expository as well as imaginative—cheers the reader as it informs; it is rich and evocative, as well as clear and economical.

**Communication.** Writing is communication, and it can be the best form of communication we have. A writer communicates when he or she accurately transfers an idea from his or her mind to the mind of a reader. To the good writer, communication implies a sense of audience and a sense of purpose. That is, in addition to upholding the principles of clarity and economy to make the reader's task easier, the writer uses syntax and vocabulary that are appropriate for the intended audience. All good writers have a sense of audience; even the most avant-garde prose stylist, intent on burning new paths, hopes to communicate, to get through to some reader.

The principle of clear and economical communication can serve as a touchstone by which teachers can evaluate writing. The principle applies to compositions written for science and social studies just as readily as it does to those written in an English or language arts course. Teachers in various disciplines may profitably consider, using student-written papers as examples, just what constitutes clear and economical communication. Bringing teachers together to discuss criteria for written work can aid standardization in grading; it also helps to break down the walls between disciplines or departments.

Such discussion has great benefits not only for teachers, who profit from mutual support and a common set of standards, but also for students. Students who find that their written work is being assessed with consistency from subject to subject can develop broader senses of their audience and purpose than those students who shape their writing to the standards of one particular teacher.

**Competency Skills**

The general touchstone of clear and economical communication is merely the beginning for a teacher of writing. The next step is to adapt that principle to classroom use. As a start we must break it down into teachable parts.

The most basic of these parts, without which clear and economical communication cannot take place, is *competency skills*:
1. Proper use of abbreviations, capitalization, and numbers
2. Proper use of case
3. Ability to construct complete sentences
4. Proper placement of modifiers
5. Proper use of parallel structure
6. Proper use of pronoun references (number and case)
7. Proper use of punctuation
8. Ability to spell correctly
9. Proper use of verb forms and subject-verb agreement
10. Proper use of verb tense sequence

At some point in teaching writing, this skills list becomes a kind of *error* list. For example, a teacher may teach not how to write complete sentences but how to avoid writing fragments or run-ons. Or a teacher is most likely to note spelling errors and require corrections. Teaching that proceeds solely from such a list is likely to become negative in tone. And, because students learn these skills through rote drill and correction, they are likely to be bored with writing.

# THE ELEMENTS OF GOOD WRITING

As teachers of writing, we cannot ignore competency skills, but we should not allow them to direct our teaching. A positive approach produces better writing than a negative one because students can become enthusiastic and committed to their development as writers. We can teach writing positively by helping students to identify and to learn to use the elements of good writing that produce clear and economical communication. These elements characterize good writing, wherever it exists.

### ELEMENTS OF GOOD WRITING

- Active voice
- Audience
- Clarity
- Coherence
- Conciseness
- Development
- Diction
- Emphasis
- Originality
- Sources
- Unity

The 11 elements, arranged alphabetically, are not parallel in importance or priority. Some of them are basic to all good writing: *clarity, coherence, diction,* and *unity*. These elements are emphasized in the early writing activities included in *Good Writing,* and you should, of course, insist on them in all student writing. Other elements, such as *active voice, audience,* and *sources,* are subtler; they are useful in the development of a writer's individual style.

A brief discussion of each of the elements follows. These discussions are intended to serve as the basis for presentations to your classes. Each of the writing units in Part Two of *Good Writing* addresses a few of the 11 elements. A number of the elements appear in several units; others appear in only one or two. Rather than teaching the elements in the abstract, you should present them as you work through the writing activities. In introducing Unit One, for example, you should discuss clarity, conciseness, diction, and emphasis.

Discussion of each element ends with a set of Questions for Students. These questions are designed both to help students to focus their attention on a particular element as they write and to guide their awareness of how well finished papers have employed that element. The questions are phrased so that you can give them directly to the class when you assign a writing activity.

## Active Voice

The active voice in a sentence commonly takes the pattern of *subject→ verb→ object*. In nongrammatical terms, we might express it by *actor→ action→ goal*:

*Max sank the eight ball in the side pocket.*

Max is the actor, sank is the action, and eight ball is the goal or recipient of the action.

The passive voice inverts the word order, placing the goal or object first and the subject or actor last.

*The eight ball was sunk in the side pocket by Max.*

For several reasons, a writer should cast most sentences in the active voice. For one thing, the active voice is more concise than the passive.

*Sandy found the ball in the woods.* (Active: 7 words)
*The ball was found in the woods by Sandy.* (Passive: 9 words)

Also, because the actor comes first and the verb form is simpler, the active voice is more vigorous and direct than the passive. The active voice helps the reader to visualize an action in the order in which it occurred. The passive voice changes that order, showing us a consequence before the actor that produced the consequence:

*A no-hitter was thrown by the great left-hander.*

As in this example, the passive hides the actor in a tacked-on prepositional phrase. Sometimes it eliminates the actor altogether.

Much jargon, particularly that produced by bureaucrats, is full of passive constructions. The passive slows down the pace of the prose and clouds the meaning:

*This is to advise you that the work which was ordered by you to have been completed by 7 June has not yet been completed. It is hoped that your forebearance will be granted in order that the construction may be finished shortly behind schedule.*

A writer may appropriately use the passive voice when the actor is unknown or when the action or goal is more important than the actor.

*The store was robbed last night.* (actor unknown)

*Michelangelo's* Pietà *was assaulted with a hammer by an art-hater.* (actor less important than goal)

Note, however, that in both of these cases one might use the active voice instead, although the emphasis would change.

*Someone robbed the store last night.*

*An art-hater with a hammer assaulted Michelangelo's* Pietà.

Expletive constructions using *there* or *it* are similar to the passive voice in that they waste words and also lack vigor and emphasis. For example:

*There is a nice old man who collects baseball cards living in that house.*

*It was the night watchman who let Susan in.*

These sentences would be clearer and more economical if they were rewritten:

*A nice old man who collects baseball cards lives in that house.*

*The night watchman let Susan in.*

*Questions for students:* How many sentences using the passive voice does your composition contain? How many expletive constructions? If you change two passive or expletive constructions to active voice or eliminate the expletives, how many words do you save? Are your new verbs different from your old ones?

## Audience

Writers must think about who will read what they write. Sometimes, as in advertising, a writer's audience is the first and most important consideration. A serious novelist, on the other hand, may be concerned less with audience than with subject matter and style. Most writers of prose fall in between: they must take into account the interrelationship between audience and subject. First of all, they must maintain a consistent point of view, or attitude, toward the subject. In most cases this point of view is neutral, or possibly slanted toward the views of the audience, so that communication does not falter because the audience is biased against the writer from the start. Writers are also concerned about tone, or the expression of their relationship with the audience. Again, the tone is often neutral; but sometimes writers adopt tones of exhortation, consolation, or even anger.

In addition to point of view and tone, a certain diction and sentence structure are appropriate for one audience and not appropriate for another. A set of rules for swimming in the pond at a day camp for eight-year-olds, for instance, should employ basic words, simple sentence structure, and an authoritative tone. An advertisement for a sugared breakfast cereal would be likely to adopt an enthusiastic point of view, a chummy tone, and trendy diction in order to attract its young audience. A politician might address a group of factory workers in a more comradely tone, with more direct diction than he or she would use at a press conference.

One way to study the effect of an awareness of one's audience is to examine advertisements. The advertisers know their audiences well, and they pitch their ad copy appropriately. Here are two examples from the magazine section of a Sunday newspaper:

> *A fresh, woody-floral blend of precious blossoms and rare mosses from the shores of the Mediterranean, enhanced with exotic touches of the Orient. In Eau de Toilette and Parfums unveiled today in a sculpted crystal flacon, Galanos is a study in true artistry, for the woman who wants the ultimate in elegance in her life!*
>
> *What are you doing for fun today?*
> *Here, in our salon, you can meet new friends while you shape up together. And lose inches without starving. It costs only $25 for six weeks of unlimited visits.*

Although both of these ads are directed to women, their sense of audience is different, and therefore so is their style. The perfume advertisement, haughty in tone, features pretentious diction and elaborate syntax, while the reducing center hopes to attract its customers with a breezy, "plain folks" approach, and with spare, informal diction and syntax.

A particular problem with teaching writing in school is that the teacher is the most logical audience for student compositions. Of course, it *is* the teacher who will read the paper, and many students study their teachers' preferences and peeves and adjust their writing accordingly. These students do have a sense of what it means to write for an audience, but it is much too limited an audience. After your students have left school, their communication may succeed or fail according to how accurately they have gauged their audience. A letter to a prospective employer, an evaluation of a technical product, or a news release about the latest meeting of the citizens' radio club will not do the job of communicating if the tone, diction, and content of the writing are not appropriate for the intended audience. Therefore, assignments that cause students to write for audiences other than the teacher (e.g., classmates, people of certain philosophical or religious beliefs, younger children, or friends of their parents) are very important.

*Questions for students:* What is your audience? Are your point of view, tone, diction, and sentence structure appropriate for that audience? Will your audience be interested in what you have to say? Why? Find some words that you believe appeal specifically to your audience.

**Clarity**

Writers achieve clarity through precision, and they achieve precision through good hard work. They must find just the right words and phrases to communicate their ideas without the reader misunderstanding. A sentence like the one below betrays a lazy writer:

*It seems the city is finally going to persecute all those parking tickets.*

The writer has mistaken persecute for prosecute and would apparently have us believe that the city is going to hale some tickets into court rather than those people who have violated the parking laws.

In addition to exact diction, writers must employ appropriate sentence construction to express their ideas without fuzziness. For example, in this sentence we know what the words mean, but we do not know what the sentence means:

*I'll bet Helen likes tennis better than you.*

Has Helen gone off to play tennis because she prefers the game to your company? Or is she simply more enthusiastic about the game than you are? The sentence is unclear.

Clarity comes from editing, with a dictionary at hand, rather than from intuition. The writer's own scrupulous examination of key terms (Does it really mean what I want it to mean?) is the first step in editing for clarity. Eliminating errors that may mislead a reader is an important part of this first editing. Asking for another opinion can be a useful second step. A reader other than the writer can point out words, phrases, and clauses that are unclear, and perhaps offer suggestions about how best to clarify them. Then, as the student rewrites, clarity improves, and, along with it, communication.

*Questions for students:* What are the three most important nouns in your composition? What are their dictionary definitions? Do the definitions agree with the idea or image that you had? Do the dictionary definitions of any three-syllable verbs you have used agree with your sense of their meanings? Draw arrows from two adverbs to the words they modify, and check the meanings of those adverbs.

## Coherence

Coherent writing sticks together. It proceeds clearly from one point to another, as it develops the central, or unifying, idea. One way that student writers may approach coherence is to follow certain structural patterns for paragraphs or compositions. For instance, a composition that describes the process of learning to ride a ten-speed bicycle has a good start toward coherence if it follows a chronological order ("First adjust the seat..."). An essay that traces the causes of the War of 1812 will be coherent if the writer presents those causes chronologically, although that approach may sacrifice emphasis upon the most significant causes of the war.

To aid coherence in students' work, emphasize and practice *transitions*. Transitions lead the reader from one idea to another. Sometimes they lead from idea to related supporting idea ("at the same time," "similarly"). At other times they help the reader to jump from one idea to a related but contrasting one ("on the other hand," "nevertheless"). By means of transitions, a writer can communicate complex ideas in a clear, sequential manner.

Here are paragraphs from two essays written by tenth-grade students:

A  *It is often said that you can tell someone's personality by the type of dog he owns. I often find this true and at times quite amusing. For example, I know one man who attended a notable "prep" school, went to Harvard, and upon graduating moved to his family's home outside of Boston. There, he acquired two dogs. Of course, they were both labs, one yellow and one black. I also know of a very pampered author living on a large estate about 20 miles from London. She's content after writing several books to stroll lazily through her garden carrying a parasol in one hand and a Pekingese in the other.*

B  *Vietnam became one of the most devastating wars, because thousands of men, mostly young, were dying for really no reason. Many men who were drafted burned their draft cards and fled to*

*Canada. Never before had people refused to fight in a war so it left a mark and changed the way Americans thought about war and itself. Music became an escape for many young people. Groups like the Beatles gained popularity. They sang about rights and drugs. The Monkees and other groups became popular because of fraud. Groups all over were trying to copy the Beatles' style. Movements were started such as civil rights and the equal rights amendment movements....*

Paragraph B lacks unity and is incoherent. Ideas either are unconnected or their connection is not signaled by transition. Paragraph A is more successful. Concrete details lend clarity, and transitions ("I often find this true," "For example," "There," "also," and several pronoun-referent pairs) help the paragraph cohere.

*Questions for students:* How many transitions have you used in your composition? (Underline them.) Are there any sentences that you could move to other positions to make better sense? (Try it.) Make a list of the ideas in your paper after you have written it. Number the list, and see what sort of development exists. Are any of the ideas out of order?

## Conciseness

Conciseness is the principal hallmark of economical writing. A concise statement does not elaborate upon an idea beyond what is necessary to communicate to an audience. Circumlocutory and verbose writing are opposites of concise writing.

| Verbose | Concise |
|---|---|
| It has come to my attention that... | I hear that... |
| bluntly worded statement | blunt statement |
| at this particular time | now |
| Regarding the subject of the washing machine that you have stated was improperly installed by us, we have reason to believe that the difficulty was occasioned by some sort of obstruction in the drainpipe located behind the machine, rather than by any fault of ours. | Your washer overflowed because your drainpipe was clogged. |

A common enemy of conciseness is redundancy, or unintended repetition. For emphasis it may sometimes be helpful to repeat an idea, but where repetition is unintentional, it clouds meaning and weakens impact.

| Verbose | Concise |
|---|---|
| *Silence was everywhere; no sound could be heard.* | *Silence was everywhere.* |
| *Applause was universal from the entire audience.* | *Applause was universal.* |
| *We were surrounded on all sides.* | *We were surrounded.* |

Some writers like to use long words and convoluted sentence construction. They may believe that the more ornate their writing is, the better it is. The only way to reach them is to show them that their prose is not readily comprehensible to an audience—any sort of audience. But, because the ornateness may grow out of a real interest in language, deal gently with them.

Many beginning writers have the opposite difficulty: they are so laconic that they communicate little if any information. They must learn to expand before you can even consider the conciseness of their expression.

Most student writers fall in the middle: sometimes they are concise and sometimes they aren't. They must learn to edit their writing to eliminate superfluity. As they do this, they will be thinking sharply about what they have said. By forcing themselves to be more concise, they may become more precise as well.

*Questions for students:* Have you used any phrases that you could replace with a single word? Or with fewer words? (Hint: Look for clichés first.) Have you overdeveloped any of your ideas—that is, said more than the reader needs to know or more than you need to say to get the ideas across? Have you repeated yourself unnecessarily?

**Development**

Every piece of writing, from a sentence to an entire volume, has an appropriate length. This length depends on how much the writer's audience needs to know. The writing should be economical, of course, but it should contain enough information to communicate effectively to the audience.

Underdeveloped writing does not communicate accurately. It is knit too loosely of unsupported generalizations and half-formed ideas. If writing lacks either sufficient detail to explain generalizations or a careful, thorough presentation of a logical sequence of ideas, a reader will be frustrated and will have difficulty understanding what the writer intends to say.

Full development (quantity, length) is just one part of an effectively developed piece of writing. A good writer also gives thought to the *method* of development. While the number of methods of development is infinite, some methods are more appropriate to certain ideas than are others. Here, again, choice of method depends on what the writer perceives as the needs of the audience, as well as the nature of the subject matter. If you were writing directions for using a fire extinguisher, for instance, you would not begin with a graceful metaphor or a historical sketch of the fire prevention industry. What your audience needs is a clear, brief list of steps. On the other hand, a numbered list of steps is not the right sort of development for a personal essay in which you hope to evoke emotion from your audience.

The composition handbooks that provide models for student analysis and emulation often arrange these models according to certain *patterns* of development. Some of the most common patterns are example, definition, process, comparison and contrast, cause and effect, and analogy. Several of the writing activities in this book are designed to help students use these patterns. Each pattern has its own characteristics. A composition about dyeing batik fabric would be developed by process; it would consist of a series of steps in chronological order. A composition comparing fashions of today with those of the 1960s might lump all details about dress of the former period into a section, explore similarities of today's styles as transition, and then contrast details in the final part.

Of course, the vast range of human ideas does not fit comfortably into a small number of fixed patterns. Unique ideas deserve unique treatment. Still, all ideas that fit into paragraphs or larger sections have in common the need for generalizations and supporting details. A writer must establish the generalization with economy and clarity and then support or illustrate it with enough details to communicate it to the audience. The number and complexity of details are determined by the education, language facility, and experience of the audience.

Using too few details is usually the problem with beginning writers. They should learn to make lists of details (not necessarily outlines) before they begin to write, and then to prune, augment, and arrange the lists as they think about their topics.

*Questions for students:* Who is your audience and what does it need to know? How many details can you find to support each of your generalizations? Is the paper long enough to give the desired full treatment of your subject? Is there a pattern that would help to assure full and clear development of your subject? If you have found a pattern, have you followed it consistently?

## Diction

Diction in writing is the writer's choice of words. A basic limitation of a writer's diction is vocabulary: a writer who has not accumulated a large working vocabulary does not have much from which to choose. Students who have read books as they were growing up should have good vocabularies. But many students have not read much, and they need to learn more words in order to communicate their ideas clearly.

Vocabulary lists or workbooks are useful, and a thesaurus provides a sense of the range of words that cluster about a concept. The thesaurus also raises the issue of *connotation*, shades of meaning that accrue through use. Words that have similar dictionary definitions may have different connotations. A writer must recognize connotative distinctions as well as more obvious denotative meanings—otherwise inappropriate diction results. But learning writers should not be afraid to reach out for new words. If some words are inappropriate, a teacher or student editor will point them out, and the writer can try other words, or try these words in another context.

A common problem for most learning writers is achieving a consistent kind of diction. Diction ranges from formal to informal and includes special kinds of language, such as slang and jargon. Students often mix slang with more formal expression:

> *Shakespeare uses the porter as an unknowing commoner who has been up half the night carousing. He makes him speak, because he is blotto, in a comic yet eerie manner.*

Or they may insert specialized jargon into a composition intended for a general audience:

*For the modern professional athlete, a sharp lawyer is a necessary interface between him and the team owner.*

Certain topics, such as a description of a dance party written for a teenage audience, may lend themselves to development that uses contemporary slang. Other topics, such as an argument against nuclear power, are more convincingly developed with formal diction. An article intended for ski buffs about the ski trails of Sugarbush Mountain can communicate well using ski jargon, while an explanation of the principles of electricity in a sixth-grade science book should not employ jargon.

In any case, the diction depends on the intended audience and the vocabulary of the writer. Once a kind of diction is established for a piece of writing, it should not be changed, except for special emphasis.

In addition to knowing enough words and using the appropriate ones, a writer must choose just the right word to communicate a certain idea, and that is the hardest job of all. Clear communication depends on precise word choice. Of course, a writer with a large vocabulary has a good start toward finding just the right words, but even that writer chooses badly sometimes. And because the job is hard, sometimes a writer settles for a vague or abstract word instead of the precise, concrete term that really fits. Words such as *thing, phase,* and *aspect* suggest that the writer needs to work harder on word selection. Careful editing, using a dictionary, will help a writer achieve clear, precise diction.

*Questions for students:* What are the most important words in your paper, the words on which the meaning hangs? (Underline them.) Are they clear, precise, and forceful? (Look them up if you are in doubt.) What kind of diction are you using? Formal? Informal? Specialized? General? Are there any words that are inappropriate to that kind of diction? (Beware of slang.)

## Emphasis

To achieve emphasis a writer manipulates words and structures in order to draw attention to important ideas. A writer who has good control of emphasis has a strong start toward achieving accurate communication with the audience. Within a sentence, a carefully chosen word or phrase can create emphasis; within a paragraph, a sentence can; within a longer piece, a paragraph can. Effective emphasis on the focal idea or ideas in a composition makes the reader pause to think.

A requisite for emphatic writing is the ability to discriminate between important ideas and subordinate or supporting ideas. Sentence drill, particularly combining activities, is the most direct way of developing this ability. Generally speaking, ideas of equal importance within the same sentence should appear in coordinate constructions: such a sentence might consist of two or more independent clauses, or several parallel phrases. On the other hand, ideas that are not roughly equal in importance should not be coordinate. Usually the important ideas should appear prominently in an independent clause, and the less important ideas in subordinate clauses or phrases.

Coordinate:

*What Eric wants is a good home; what he needs are foster parents who care.*

Subordinate:

*Molly can't drive us tonight because her sister needs the car.*

Practice with sentence combining trains writers to weigh the relative importance of ideas and to cast them in appropriate coordinate or subordinate constructions. The disciplined thought that such activities produce has the further benefit of reinforcing the habit of thinking critically while editing.

Writers achieve emphasis through the use of a variety of methods:

Diction: use of a startling word or phrase.

*Future generations will look back with amazement if war is averted.*[6]

—JOHN FOSTER DULLES

Figure: use of an attention-getting original metaphor or image.

*Within six weeks we were to find ourselves alone, almost disarmed, with triumphant Germany and Italy at our throats, with the whole of Europe in Hitler's power, and Japan glowering on the other side of the globe.*[7]

—SIR WINSTON CHURCHILL

Placement: setting the focal idea abruptly at the beginning or at the end. The periodic sentence delays the most important idea until the very end of the sentence.

> *The only thing that was wrong now, really, was the sound of the place, an unfamiliar nervous sound of the outboard motors.*[8]
> —E. B. WHITE

Order: changing the usual word order, usually by inverting the normal sentence structure or by inserting an interrupter to break the rhythm of the sentence.

> *As revealing as his rooms are the presents a man gives.*[9]
> —MARYA MANNES

Repetition: repeating important words or phrases or repeating the structure of phrases or clauses. (Unintentional repetition, of course, can cause confusion because it emphasizes ideas that do not need emphasis.)

> *For decades the building process soaked up all available skilled labor; for decades the townspeople stepped around pits in the streets, clambered over ropes and piles of timber, breathed mortar dust and slept and woke to the crashing noise of construction.*[10]
> —ERIC SEVAREID

Contrast: juxtaposing contrasting ideas in the same sentence, usually in two independent clauses joined with *but* or *yet*, or in other parallel units.

> *We have vowed that we shall not see space filled with weapons of mass destruction, but with instruments of knowledge and understanding.*[11]
> —JOHN F. KENNEDY

Writers can combine these methods, along with other ways of achieving emphasis, in a single sentence, one that forces the audience to slow down and ponder the idea.

> *Upon each of the three faces was written a passionate envy of the old, old ways which they had chosen to deny and deride and which could, now, never be theirs.*[12]
> —ANNE SINCLAIR MEHDEVI

An emphatic paragraph in a longer piece can call attention to itself, just as a sentence can. A very short paragraph, perhaps just a single sentence, leaps out at a reader from among longer paragraphs. A paragraph with end emphasis makes a reader pause and perhaps even review the paragraph.

Any sort of vague writing detracts from emphasis. Particular enemies of emphasis are fuzzy diction, verbosity or redundancy, passive voice, and incoherent development.

Unemphatic paragraph:

> In "The Rime of the Ancient Mariner," Coleridge's use of certain points of nature seems to express the importance of religion in the poem. The albatross and the rain scenes can each be interpreted as having specific relationships to certain ideas of religion.

Here emphasis blurs because the writing is ambiguous, repetitious, and unemphatic.

Paragraph with initial emphasis:

> The message of Coleridge's "The Rime of the Ancient Mariner" is clear: man should love and revere all of God's creatures. Coleridge transmits this message in two ways. First, he shows a man who violates the message, and second, he relates the resulting atrocities of the man's punishment.

This writer has focused his paper on a clear theme. Furthermore, this focal paragraph indicates how he will develop the composition by examining in turn violation and punishment.

End emphasis:

> Through folly and boredom, through terror and agony, Coleridge attains at last what all men need: wisdom and love.

With its parallel structure and climax at the end, the sentence calls attention to itself and to its ideas.

*Questions for students:*   What are the most important ideas in the paper? Are they prominent or hidden? Look at the sentences that state those ideas: are they emphatic? Where are the major ideas in your paragraph? Are they clearly stated? Are the sentences that express them emphatic? If not, can you rewrite them to make a reader pause (not because of awkwardness but because of unique phrasing, diction, or structure)? Have you written emphatic sentences that express lesser ideas or subordinate details and might confuse the audience about what is important?

## Originality

Good writing is original. Trite phrases, dead metaphors, old slogans—these bore a reader and leave no impression. On the other hand, a fresh, emphatic structure, or an arresting metaphor, or a sharp word used properly in a new context arouses the interest of a reader and makes the writer's idea memorable.

Variety is a component of originality. Line after line of similarly structured sentences or a succession of similarly shaped paragraphs stultifies the development of ideas and prevents emphasis. As long as the writer's point of view is consistent throughout the piece of writing, and as long as the variation in the elements of writing aids rather than opposes emphasis, variety of length and form contributes to the readability and memorable originality of the piece.

Of the two routes to originality in writing, one is essentially negative: avoidance of the worn and obvious. In editing, a writer must cut out clichés ("sadder but wiser," "last but not least," "adding insult to injury") and dead metaphors ("white as snow," "straight as an arrow") and replace them with vivid, exact terms. While editing, the writer can also spot monotonous similarity and oversimplicity in sentence structure and can rewrite sentences to achieve emphasis through a structure that is not as familiar to the reader.

The other route to originality is invention, and this route is harder to follow. It is one thing to edit a piece of writing in order to put pep in dull parts; it is quite another thing to compose with the imagination that produces originality in the first place. Imagination cannot be inculcated; but it can be encouraged. The teacher should promote originality in student writing by praising and rewarding imaginative efforts—even when those efforts are not wholly successful. Originality extends beyond diction and sentence structure. A student may employ a certain form in an original way (a poem in answer to an expository question, for instance), and, as long as the usage is original, the writer should be rewarded.

The imagination can produce vivid original effects through figurative language. A fresh metaphor or simile gives life to a sentence or paragraph and makes it different from anything the reader has read before.

In the following excerpts writers have achieved originality through figurative language, structure, variety, and precise diction. Behind each example lies an active imagination.

*Through the tangle of verbiage, the idea of "common cause" skitters like a shy bird.*[13]

—E. B. WHITE

*She sat stiffly, alone in the stern of the boat and the constraint and trouble seemed to hedge her in, to reach her across the sea from those dotted figures on the headland.*[14]

—RUMER GODDEN

> Question mark for a world it baffles, Israel is a question also in relation to its own history. I make it mine, just as I make mine Israel's determination to transform the hate imposed upon it into a craving for solidarity with the world.[15]
> —ELIE WIESEL
>
> Meanwhile the carnivores lifted forks that appeared to have grown heavy with their cargo of turkey and trimmings.[16]
> —MARY McCARTHY

*Questions for students:* Are there any clichés or dead metaphors in your writing? Is your opening paragraph original, or have you often begun this way before? Have you used original figurative language to make your ideas vivid?

**Sources**

Often good writers borrow from sources (the writings of others). These borrowings serve two chief functions: (1) use of a source can buttress a writer's argument by drawing on the expertise of another and (2) borrowing a witty line or a choice turn of phrase from another writer can enliven one's prose and also provide a refreshing variety of voice or point of view.

But the effective use of sources is not simple. The first step is to recognize when the use of a source is appropriate. The writer must also learn how to locate apt sources. Then the writer must be able to incorporate the source gracefully into his or her own writing. Finally, and most importantly—for it separates proper source use from plagiarism—the writer must accurately follow the conventions that acknowledge the borrowing of material from a source.

Where in a piece of writing are quotations from sources appropriate? Throughout, but we often find them at the beginning:

> "No one could have known Max who did not understand what Windsor, or Vermont in general, meant for him, the deep stake in the old rural America from which the foreground of his life was in many of its elements so far removed," Van Wyck Brooks wrote in **Scenes and Portraits**. Practically all of Perkins's life was spent in New York City or its suburbs but the tart values of New England were the essence of his character.[17]
> —A. SCOTT BERG

or at the end of sections:

> Amado Vazquez loved his country. Amado Vazquez loved his family. Amado Vazquez loved orchids. "You want to know how I

*feel about the plants,"* he said as I was leaving. *"I'll tell you. I will die in orchids."*[18]

—JOAN DIDION

In his biography of editor Maxwell Perkins, A. Scott Berg uses a quotation from a book by Perkins's closest friend to introduce a section on the editor's New England roots. Joan Didion ends her portrait of a little-known orchid grower with the grower's own words, words that neatly summarize his passion for his vocation.

While they make good openings and good conclusions, sources are also used in the body of a piece of writing. They are especially effective in argument or persuasive writing.

To find useful sources, students must read. In preparing reports, of course, they read authoritative sources, some parts of which they will want to quote. For sources on any specific subject, from love to lettuce, reference works (the most widely available is Bartlett's *Familiar Quotations*) are helpful. In addition to quotations from written sources, writers use quoted speech (as Joan Didion does), television commercials, secondhand stories— whatever they feel is appropriate for and interesting to their audiences.

Once they have found appropriate sources, writers must reproduce them accurately and punctuate them properly. Use of three dots ( . . . ) for ellipsis is useful when the whole quotation is bulky or when part of it is irrelevant; but the ellipsis should not change the intended meaning of the source.

Attribution of a quotation to its source is important. Beginning writers often plunk down a statement in quotation marks and let it speak for itself. This practice irritates a reader, who wants to know where the statement came from and what authority lies behind it. Attributive transitions, such as "The pollster George Gallup claims that 'Americans . . .' " or " ' . . . the two major political parties,' according to a Gallup poll," inform the audience and smooth the prose so that the quotation does not jar.

Of course, writers must acknowledge their sources for another reason: to avoid plagiarizing, or representing someone else's ideas or words as the writer's own. In a relatively formal paper, this acknowledgement takes the form of a footnote (and perhaps it is also included in a bibliography); in a short or informal piece of writing, attribution within the text is enough. The intricate conventions of footnoting and bibliography are many; the standard guide is the *MLA Style Sheet*.

*Questions for students:* Will a quotation provide an interesting and helpful lead? Can you use one or more sources to support your central contention? Are the quotations you use accurate, properly punctuated, and clearly attributed to their sources, both in the text and (if appropriate) in footnotes and a bibliography?

## Unity

Unity in writing is faithful adherence to a central idea. In a sentence, unity is the expression of a single complete thought; in a paragraph, unity is the development of the topic idea; in a longer piece, unity is development of the thesis statement. The chief foe of unity is irrelevance. Ideas that do not bear on the central idea send the reader off on confusing tangents and blunt the impact of the writing.

Achievement of unity is vital, and it is not difficult. The writer has two devices to aid in creating unity: an organizing statement and an outline.

In the case of a paragraph, the organizing statement is the *topic sentence*. It should state the central idea and indicate generally how the paragraph will develop. For example:

> *The helmet is the most important piece of protective gear in ice hockey.*

This simple topic sentence not only expresses a central idea, it also indicates that the paragraph will deal with several points, all related to that idea:
- what the helmet is
- why it is so important
- how it protects
- why this protection is necessary in ice hockey

A writer who can construct clear, organizing topic sentences finds it easy to achieve paragraph unity since the topic sentence tightly controls development, rendering irrelevancy unlikely.

Not that a topic sentence must be dull or formulaic. This topic sentence

> *Youth and beauty are this singer's chief assets.*

may indeed mean that the paragraph will discuss the singer's youth and beauty, but the implied topic idea is that the singer cannot sing, and the writer might use "youth and beauty" to lead into that idea. A topic sentence like this one does not state the central idea—but that central idea is clear in the mind of the writer and clear to a reader who is thinking.

The *thesis statement* organizes a composition as the topic sentence organizes the paragraph. For example:

> *The purposes of pruning are various: to keep plants healthy, to restrict or to promote growth, to encourage bloom, or to repair damage.*[19]
>
> —JOHN PHILIP BAUMGARDT

This clear and unremarkable thesis statement shows exactly where the writer is going and tells us that his unified development of the purposes of pruning plants will have four parts.

> *Mathematics is in many ways the most elaborated and sophisticated of the sciences—or so it seems to me, as a mathematician.*[20]
>
> —J. BRONOWSKI

This thesis statement sets up a possible pattern of development: definition of elaborated and sophisticated; and the relation of these terms to mathematics, and, in comparison, to other sciences. Bronowski's thesis statement also establishes the tone that he will employ throughout the piece: somewhat formal, but personal.

In any piece, the *tone*, or the relationship between the writer and the audience, must be consistent. If the diction varies from slang to intellectualisms, or the syntax from bare to convoluted, confusion and disunity result. Sometimes, however, a writer will abruptly shift tone for emphasis, as in the example that follows; but this is a risky device for beginning writers.

> *One of the curiosities of Communism is that an ideology founded on the inexorable influence of economics should do so poorly in delivering the goods.*[21]
>
> —HENRY KISSINGER

The apparently intentional jarring of tone here ("inexorable influence" versus "delivering the goods") reinforces the thrust of the piece as set forth in the thesis statement: that the high-flown rhetoric of Communism belies its inability to succeed in daily life. The piece goes on to maintain its unity by comparing rhetoric and performance.

It pays to labor over a topic sentence or a thesis statement. By presenting the connected ideas to be developed, the statement creates unity and makes the direction of development clear. One point: the topic sentence or thesis statement need not come first; in fact, it may be omitted from the finished piece. But, because it helps to focus and organize ideas, the writer should write one, even if he or she doesn't use it in the end.

Outlining helps to check both unity and coherence. Some writers like to make formal outlines; others merely jot down ideas and then begin to write. Both formal outlines and informal lists allow the writer to scan the ideas and judge, on the one hand, whether or not they all pertain to the central idea (checking for unity), and, on the other, whether or not they are in a logical order (checking for coherence).

*Questions for students:* Does your writing have a single, clearly discernible central idea? Is this idea stated in a way that organizes the rest of the paragraph or composition? Have you checked to eliminate irrelevant details?

## DEVELOPING A TEACHING STRATEGY

The 11 elements of good writing are most useful in the context of an organized program for teaching writing as clear and economical communication. Such a program is included in this book. But before considering that program, let us consider some general and specific strategies for teaching writing. These strategies are helpful not only in using the writing program presented in Part Two of this book, but also in other situations in which writing is taught.

Each of us writes uniquely. What one student needs from a teacher may be quite different from another's need. For instance, Mary has lots of great ideas but a mind that moves light-years ahead of her pen. She loves to write, but her writing is incoherent and she is frustrated that others don't understand her. Bill is another case. He feels that writing is not for him. In class he will produce barely a sentence. But he is clever and inventive. He must overcome his block and just get going. And then there are Rachel, Harry, John, Willy, Denise, Sue—maybe 30 in an hour, 150 in a day.

Because student needs and abilities are so diverse, a teacher must avoid the temptation to use a single approach to teaching writing. Theories of teaching abound, but it is unlikely that any one theory will work well for all students. Most of these theories lie between two extremes, which, at the risk of oversimplification, we might call *planning* and *spontaneity*.

## Planning

Planning postulates that writing is a logical, disciplined endeavor. By careful and organized thought, a writer decides what to say, and the process of writing consists of transcribing those thoughts onto paper. The steps in this process are three: decide what you want to say, figure out how to say it, and write it down. While there may be latitude in the writer's use of tools of expression, such as choice of sentence structure or selection of a useful figure of speech, the written product contains all of the ideas that the writer chose to include before beginning to write, only those ideas, and those ideas in a predetermined order.

Teaching based on this philosophy of writing emphasizes *prewriting* and ordered thought. The writer carefully limits the topic and makes an outline that lists ideas in a sensible organizational scheme (least to most important or chronologically first to last, for example). Perhaps the writer selects patterns for these ideas: a cause-and-effect paragraph; or a "frame" for the composition, in which the opening idea is recapitulated at the end. All of these steps are completed before the writer begins to write the composition itself. The writer considers the audience while preparing to write: the reader deserves to receive the information in a logical, easy-to-understand form.

The planning philosophy is attractive to teachers for two principal reasons. First, it lends itself to structure. A whole class may be led together through the steps of composition, beginning with the selection and narrowing of one topic and ending with a detailed outline. From that point each student can write a composition from the common outline, and each composition is likely to be well organized and full of ideas (though not the individual student's own ideas). Or the teacher with a lighter load may deal with students individually all along the way, checking the satisfactory progress of each one at every step—topic, notes, outline, and rough draft.

Second, planning can be a useful tool for building confidence. The student progresses step by step with each paper; there is guidance at each step, and reinforcement to provide a sense of improvement from paper to paper. In fact, the poor writer may be able to make large gains in unity and coherence at the start by following, even ploddingly, formulas and models that produce a basic level of competence.

## Spontaneity

Those who argue for spontaneity, the other extreme, see planning as a sham. They claim that professional writers do not work in such an ordered, mechanical fashion. Advocates of spontaneity say that writing generates ideas instead of merely transcribing them. One idea leads to another, and, as a composition grows, it achieves its own organic coherence. Planning limits thought and cripples writing. Devices such as outlines and paragraph models hamper expression rather than aiding it. Expression is primary; consideration of audience is secondary.

Teachers who espouse this philosophy of writing lack the structural devices of their planning counterparts, but they rejoice in that lack. Instead, they strive to start their students *doing* some writing, any kind of writing.

Many teachers like this approach to writing because it draws on a student's imagination. A learning writer can take pride in effort and originality. The writing process is constantly novel; it keeps the student's mind active, generating and developing ideas.

## Flexibility

Although proponents of both of these extremes do exist, we should recognize that both points of view are oversimple and incomplete: neither really accounts for the way all people write. Professional writers do plan, though perhaps not with the limits that a classroom teacher might impose. On the other hand, overplanning certainly stifles spontaneity, and, if all writing were wholly planned, we would have a lot of dull writing—and very little of what we think of as literature. Imagination and spontaneity are vital to good writing, as is a modicum of thought before the writer begins.

A useful philosophy for teaching writing must recognize that most writers operate somewhere on the continuum between planning and spontaneity. Furthermore, a writer may move along that continuum in one direction or another, impelled by one or more of a number of forces: sophistication, experience, specific purpose, affinity for subject matter, confidence, and so forth. In any class of students, some will deal more effectively with an assignment that requires a good deal of planning, while others will prosper with a more spontaneous approach. The key is to vary the assignments. Give students a feel for the range of ways to do a piece of writing; gradually they will find some strategies that suit them as individuals. The various writing activities in this book incorporate both planning and spontaneous approaches to writing.

**Making Assignments**

Flexibility in teaching writing implies flexibility in making assignments. Assignments may take various forms and shapes. But whether a teacher wishes to elicit spontaneous writing, planned writing, or something in between, the quality of student responses depends in substantial part upon the *clarity* and the amount of *prescription*, or directions, of the assignment.

As teachers of writing we must work as hard on our assignments as students work on their thesis statements, because so much depends on them. Once you know what content you wish an assignment to cover, you must decide how prescriptive it will be —how much direction it will provide for the students.

Assignments should be more or less prescriptive according to the abilities of the students, your desire for specific information, and the expected complexity of the student response. If you teach an advanced placement English class that has learned how to control the scope of a topic and to select and order material, you might give a lightly prescriptive assignment. If the assigned task has several parts, or if you expect mastery of specific information, your assignment should be heavily prescriptive.

Here are examples of lightly and heavily prescriptive assignments on the same subject:

A *Discuss Fitzgerald's symbolism in* **The Great Gatsby**.

B *A symbol is an object that represents something else in addition to itself. Explain what the green light on Daisy Buchanan's dock means to Gatsby, and then what it means to Fitzgerald. Your composition should be four to six paragraphs long.*

Note that B will produce similar responses (and be easier to grade), whereas A allows for much more variety in the responses, both in content and in organization.

As an example of the middle ground in degree of prescription, here is an assignment that falls between A and B above:

C  *Choose one important symbol from* The Great Gatsby *and explain what it means to one of the characters and to the author.*

**Be Certain Assignments Are Clear.**  You rarely err by making assignments too prescriptive; students need direction until they become accomplished writers. But it is important to keep in mind that good prescriptive assignments possess three types of clarity:

*Clarity of language.*  Clarity begins with verbs. Here are some verbs commonly used in assignments: *discuss, trace, explain, comment on, justify, explore, list, explicate.* Note that some of these verbs are without direction—*comment on* or *discuss* do not really indicate what the writer is to do. On the other hand, a verb such as *trace*, which calls for chronological, cause-effect development of a topic, or *list*, which implies that the student is to supply a number of examples or details, do give some direction. If you intend a degree of prescription, find the precise verb that defines the appropriate task.

Clarity also requires definition of key nouns. An assignment such as "Analyze the character of Billy Budd" is potentially confusing. Although the verb provides some direction by suggesting that the topic should be broken down into several parts, *character* allows more than one meaning. The assignment could be calling for analysis of the personality traits of Billy Budd, or an analysis of Melville's development of this character, or even some sort of discussion of the nature of the story itself. Other examples of the sorts of nouns or noun phrases that can cause confusion are *environment, socioeconomic conditions,* and *story*: all are broad and require a phrase or clause of explanation (if a more precise term is not available).

Although fuzzy assignments are most often the result of verb and noun problems, other parts of speech are important, too. Check each word in your assignments.

*Clarity of scope.*  The scope of an assignment has two senses. It denotes the expected length, and sometimes the form, of the student's response: "in complete sentences for each," "in a paragraph," "limit your composition to three to five paragraphs." Scope also sets limits for the content the student is expected to deal with: "isolationism from 1912-1916" and "imagery in the first quatrain." Clear indication of scope helps to prevent disorganized, unfocused responses. It also aids in establishing clear criteria for grading.

*Clarity of sequence.* A development by specific steps is appropriate for some assignments. An assignment that indicates the order of these steps benefits the coherence of the response. The assignment below provides a clear sense of order.

> Identify the figure of speech in line four, and explain what two things are implicitly compared. Then select and similarly explain two explicit figurative comparisons elsewhere in the poem.

And this is the same assignment with vague sequence:

> Find one implicit and two explicit figures of speech in the poem, and show how they work.

**Discuss Assignments.** Early in their development as writers, students need more than clear assignments. It is important to spend class time discussing each assignment. Explain the organizational principle involved, if a specific principle is called for. In an assignment such as "Compare, in a three-page composition, Hemingway's Robert Jordan and Kesey's Henry Stamper," the principle, *comparison*, is named; but in other assignments the class will have to determine an appropriate method of development. "Discuss the concept of justice in *Enemy of the People*" calls for development by definition and supporting examples; "Trace the loss of King Lear's dignity in Acts I and II" suggests a cause-and-effect structure.

But don't be too dogmatic about fixed structure. You will probably receive some good papers that do not fit the most obvious structures and some bad ones that do. Your discussion of the possibilities for a paper's organization should show students that organization is a concrete task that they can perform and that, by thinking of ways to build the paper, they will be seeing the scope of it from beginning to end.

A helpful exercise is to have the class as a whole create a mock or trial paper, using a topic with a shape similar to that of the topic you are assigning. Their comparison of two protagonists, for instance, could be preceded by a comparison of two movie actors or two members of the class. This comparison might begin with a generalization embodying the similarities and differences of the two persons who are being compared: "Although Ernie Slivovitz is intelligent and resolute, in times of stress the daring and cunning of Ronnie Vandergrumph are more likely to bring results." Then the generalization should be supported by illustrative examples. Someone will probably introduce an irrelevant example or say something about one that can't be compared with the other. Show the class how these ideas do not fit.

Weak, incoherent papers result from a fuzzy sense of purpose. By assigning a clear topic and an appropriate length for the paper and then going over both ideas and organization in class, you help your writers to sharpen their sense of purpose and to control their material. After a while, however, they should learn to repeat this process by themselves.

**Narrow the Topic.** When you assign a broad topic (e.g., "Shakespeare's *Hamlet*") to an inexperienced class, you create big trouble. If your students are not used to narrowing their own topics, they will write papers which are remarkable for their diversity but lamentable for their lack of order and focus.

The intermediate step between assigning a strictly defined topic explained carefully in class and letting the students fend for themselves is to spend class time narrowing a broad topic. The topic might be one that you have given or a free choice by your students. In any case, it will demand shaping. Start with a general idea of subject matter and of the scope of the paper. Then narrow the general subject. Here are two examples of the process:

| SCOPE | TOPIC A | TOPIC B |
|---|---|---|
| Volumes | Shakespeare | Sports |
|  | Shakespeare's *Hamlet* | Team sports |
|  | *Hamlet* as tragedy | Basketball |
|  | Tragic isolation in *Hamlet* | Offensive basketball |
| A book | Tragic isolation of Hamlet (the character) | Fast-break offense |
| 3–5 pp. | Tragic isolation of Hamlet in Act III | Starting a fast break |
| 1 p. | Tragic isolation of Hamlet as seen in III, i, 56–88 | Rebounding to start a fast break |

Practice this over and over with both broad literary topics and student ideas. The exercise produces fast-paced classes that students enjoy. Students are quick to spot suggestions that are out of place (too broad, too narrow, or not a part of the logical narrowing progression). Such practice helps them eliminate fuzzy sprawl from their own papers.

**Helping Students Plan**

Whether most of your assignments require thorough planning (notes, thesis statement, outline, rough draft, smooth draft) or not, you should give your students some practice in these skills. Remember, however, that each writer is unique, with unique needs. Providing a set process for writing will help to banish uncertainty about how to proceed for your less confident students. Some will find planning much to their liking and will use it whenever they write. Others may find the process tedious, but will nonetheless fall back on it when they are having trouble organizing their ideas.

Are you a stickler for form? Do you insist that notes take a particular shape and that outlines follow only a certain pattern? If so, you are reinforcing the idea that writing involves discipline. But you may also be inhibiting your students, who may find forms other than yours more helpful.

Show the class a *range* of useful ways of taking notes, or making outlines, or writing rough drafts; most composition handbooks show several forms. Have them select one form and be true to it. Or they may prefer to develop their own forms. If the forms work for them, fine. But your students should remember that notes and outlines are meant to help them communicate—so they must be able to read their own notes easily and to make good use of those notes when they write.

**Check Notes and Outlines.**  Spend time in class going over students' notes and outlines. Put some on the board or overhead projector. The chief problems with notes are *inaccuracy* (careless quotation or careless use of quotation marks and misleading paraphrase); *incompleteness* (which results in out-of-context statements); and *inadequate bibliographical information* for footnotes and bibliography.

Most outlines will contain examples of *faulty parallelism*: an important idea placed under a lesser one or unequal ideas given equal development. Faulty parallelism leads to inappropriate emphasis in the written paper. Also, some items in most outlines will be *out of order*. As the whole outline is put in front of the class, the students and the writer will be able to spot misordered items that produce incoherence.

Here is part of an outline that demonstrates both faulty parallelism and misplaced information:

THESIS: Shirley Jackson's "The Lottery" shows how blindly following a ritual can produce inhuman behavior.
  I. Setting
     A. A small town—unspecified (universality)
     B. June 27
        1. springtime: irony?
        2. possible fertility rite
     C. Atmosphere—festive, enthusiastic (or casual?)
 II. Characters
     A. Mr. Summers (sig. names?)
     B. Mr. Graves
     C. The Delacroix's
     D. Old Man Warner
     E. The Hutchinsons, Tessie
III. Ritual
     A. Reasons
        1. there's always been a lottery
        2. "Lottery in June, corn be heavy soon."
        3. other towns have changed or stopped
     B. Practice
        1. black box—sig.?
        2. each family draws
        3. stoning to death
 IV. Foreshadowing
     A. Ominous statements

The outline does suggest a good bit of information, yet a paper written from it will be a poor development of the thesis statement. Note that the stated intention is to show the effect of following a ritual on the behavior of characters in the story. Yet the outline opens with material on setting—essentially irrelevant, not to the story, but to the thesis. Section IB goes especially far off the track, suggesting an idea not clearly present in the story. Then the outline disposes of the characters in a random or chronological way before coming to the ritual—an inversion of the logical order suggested by the thesis statement. Section III is important, but out of balance. IIIA (Reasons) is less important (again, to this paper's thesis, not to the story) than IIIB (Practice); and within both A and B ideas are out of balance and probably out of order. Section IV (perhaps discussed in class) does not belong in the paper at all.

This is a sloppy outline, apparently written with little thought for the thesis or for the unity and coherence of the final paper. As it stands, it is almost useless, although its writer might be able to sort it out and make a more useful outline from it. Your class can fix it, too; by sharpening the focus on the thesis statement, they can rewrite it with the elements in order and in balance with each other.

Practice in analyzing the logic of outlines will help the students learn a key lesson: when they write, they must learn to keep the thesis, or central idea, in mind as they prepare their own outlines and papers. A good outline will give their paper a decent chance to be cohesive.

## Editing and Revision

Rough drafts need editing and revision. Make sure that students do not view drafts as something to show to the teacher and then copy verbatim. When students hand in their drafts, skim to find areas that need work. Do not mark small things, such as spelling errors. Use some class time for workshops in which students can edit the drafts. Demand, where appropriate, large alterations: chunks crossed out, paragraphs shifted from one place to another, transitions inserted, a new conclusion written, or an opening rephrased. It is the responsibility of the writer to edit for syntax, punctuation, and spelling errors.

As students are editing their papers, spot check to be sure that they are making helpful changes. When you are satisfied by effort and improvement in the rough draft, students can begin the final draft.

***More Editing and Revision.*** Even the final draft is not final. In goes the paper to you, and back it comes to the writer. You will have marked some errors and some places where still more revision is needed, for effective communication or for a smoother style.

Then the writer edits and rewrites again. The demand to rewrite affects the writer's view of the writing process. Students learn that they cannot dash off a paper, set it on your desk, and say, "There! Now I'm done with that!" They should be proud of their work and satisfied that they handed it in on time. But they shouldn't think they're done with it.

The process goes on. The paper, like the writer, is on the way. It is not perfect, and, although it can never attain perfection, it can be better and better. Writing is partly a matter of *refinement*, of sharpening—first ideas, then paragraphs, sentences, phrases, and words. The major part of this refinement has occurred when the students hand in their papers, but a second opinion (yours) may point out places in the papers where editing is necessary or might be helpful.

Rarely will a wholly rewritten paper be necessary. Your students can probably learn more from correcting a few specific mistakes, or editing one or two ungainly sentences, than they can from the large and unfocused task of rewriting the whole paper. And, after a while, rewriting makes the paper go stale.

There are three principles to apply here. First, hand the papers back *soon*, while the labor of composition is still fresh for the writers, and they are still feeling some enthusiasm for their efforts. Second, don't demand too much of the revisions. A writer will quickly grow to hate a paper on which his or her efforts have apparently been useless. In most cases, one rewrite is enough; if the product is still not satisfactory, the student should try again on the next paper. Third, spend class time checking rewrites. Praise those that show effort and improvement. Make "before" and "after" comparisons of some successful revisions.

**Let Students Edit Each Other.** In some classroom situations, it is feasible for students to work together on editing their papers. As Daniel Fader points out in *Hooked on Books* (New York: Berkley, 1977), this process provides both efficiency and enthusiasm.

Although groups of other sizes are possible, an ideal number for students working together is three. The following scheme for editing in triads requires 30 to 60 minutes (not necessarily at one sitting) depending on the ability and efficiency of the students and the lengths of the papers. This process produces useful results: (1) quick feedback from two sources; (2) editing by someone other than the writer; (3) revision of the paper (though not a total rewrite); and (4) an evaluation of the revision as well as of the original.

### EDITING IN TRIADS

I. **Preview and range finding.** Students skim each other's papers to engage their minds and compare papers. They read rapidly and do not talk.
>  A reads B's paper, then C's.
>  B reads C's paper, then A's.
>  C reads A's paper, then B's.

II. **Editing.** The reader/editor now circles errors, underlines awkward phrases or clauses, and makes telegraphic marginal suggestions. At the end of the editing there is a brief, quiet question-and-answer period when the writer gets his or her paper back.
>  A edits B's paper.
>  B edits C's paper.
>  C edits A's paper.

III. **Revision.** Writers correct errors and rework papers to improve awkward spots pointed out by the editors. Again, quiet talk between writer and editor is allowed.
>  A revises own paper with C's help.
>  B revises own paper with A's help.
>  C revises own paper with B's help.

IV. **Evaluation.** Evaluator reads the revised paper and writes notes for oral evaluation. The oral evaluations proceed one at a time.
>  A evaluates C's paper.
>  B evaluates A's paper.
>  C evaluates B's paper.

Such a process gives students a chance to work together toward a common goal: improving papers before they come before the eye of the final evaluator—you.

# PART TWO

A Writing Program

## Introduction to the Program

The 12 writing units that follow have two aims: to develop students' awareness of the elements of good writing and to provide a variety of activities suited to a wide range of student writers. In general, the units move from sentence drill, narration, and description to the complexities of analysis and argument.

The presentation of the elements and skills is not strictly sequential. Development of a concept such as *audience* in several ways and at different points during the program provides reinforcement. Also, while some students will learn best what audience is through studying advertisements (Unit Six), others will respond to a direct problem-solving approach (Unit Eight).

Be sure to preview each unit thoroughly before you teach it. Some of the units contain a great deal of material; you may wish to rearrange, partially delete, or augment the activities, depending on the needs of your own class. Although each unit includes a specific sequence and concrete directions, a flexible approach to writing suggests that you may want to make changes appropriate to your class's needs.

## Structure of the Writing Units

Each unit consists of the following parts: discussion, preliminary writing, prewriting, marking guidelines, samples, and comments.

***Discussion.*** The several discussions in each unit contain information for presentation to the class: warm-ups, definitions, illustrations, and brainstorming objectives. The discussions center on the various elements of good writing explored in Part One. You will probably wish to supplement what the discussion sections have to say about specific elements with material from Part One, where the elements receive fuller treatment and where additional examples are available. For example, when you are teaching a unit that emphasizes *sources*, refer to the entry for sources in Part One. In addition to providing more detail, that entry concludes with Questions for Students. These questions are especially useful for students who have difficulty understanding how a particular element functions in their own writing; you might wish to include these questions routinely in the discussions.

Follow-up discussions assess the results of writing activities and prepare students for the major writing assignment.

***Preliminary Writing.*** Each of these sections presents a short writing activity that gives practice in the skills necessary for the larger writing assignment that follows. Some of the activities are replicas in miniature, simplified, of the larger assignment. Most are appropriate for assignment as homework. A subsequent discussion describes what to do when students bring their preliminary writing to class.

***Prewriting.*** Prewriting exercises, unlike some of the preliminary writing, are always directly related to the major writing assignment. These activities help students to:

⋄ brainstorm for ideas
⋄ focus their topics and suit them to a specified length
⋄ organize their ideas for efficient, emphatic presentation

Work through most of the prewriting activities in class so that students can take notes, ask questions, and help each other.

***Writing.*** The writing assignment (or two assignments, in Units Eight through Ten) is the culmination of the discussions and activities that precede it. When you give the assignment, relate it to earlier material in the unit. Make sure that students are aware of deadlines and the form papers are to take.

The writing in Units One and Two is short: it consists of paragraph combinations and a series of unrelated paragraphs. The point to make early on is that quality, not quantity, is paramount. None of the writing assignments, in fact, is very long; economy of expression is one goal, and another is the clarity that results from a competent and confident handling of a limited subject.

***Marking Guidelines.*** By asking yourself certain questions about each paper, you can determine how successfully students have incorporated into their papers those elements of good writing that each unit emphasizes. The guidelines for marking each writing assignment consist of a series of such questions. Of course, in marking papers you should not limit yourself to the guideline questions; ideas, mechanics, and organization are important, too. But comments that praise success in achieving mastery of the emphasized material provide effective reinforcement.

***Samples.*** These are unedited student papers, written by tenth- and eleventh-graders in a composition course based on the writing program. The papers are generally strong, but they were selected because they demonstrate a range of approaches to the writing assignments rather than simply because they are good writing. You can use them as touchstones by which to judge the quality of your students' work. They are also appropriate for use as models. Unlike the work of professional writers, these samples are within the range of most student writers, who may be encouraged by reading them.

**Comments.** The brief comments that follow the samples describe how well and in what way the writer of the sample has been able to incorporate the elements that the unit teaches. The comments are intended to be objective and concrete and focus on the overall construction of the paper rather than the mechanics.

### Teaching the Units

Several general remarks about the writing units may be helpful. First, the types of writing activities provide a variety of ways to approach writing in order to serve a diverse group of writers; there is no single "system." As you teach the units, keep in mind that practice in the elements of good writing is the guiding force behind this program rather than a traditional graduated sequence of assignments.

Next, it is important that students see the culminating writing assignments in the units as parts of a process rather than as the only segments of the units that "count"—that determine their grade. To this end you can give grades for all activities, and also grade the rough draft, final draft, and editing improvement of the major assignment.

Although the writing units contain a large amount of detail, additional tasks are helpful. For instance, many teachers will want to see a rough draft for each writing assignment. In an effective writing program, students spend significant time editing their work. Editing is built into some of the activities presented here, but it should be a matter of course in the larger writing assignments as well. As they do in preliminary activities, students may exchange papers and edit each other. At times a wholesale revision is appropriate; at other times students will need to rewrite only certain sentences or paragraphs.

The units will fit into different kinds of courses in different ways. For courses devoted in major part to writing, for example, the units can constitute a complete syllabus. The units are also suitable for occasional or selective use within an existing English language arts or social studies curriculum.

# UNIT ONE
# COMBINING SENTENCES

### ELEMENTS OF GOOD WRITING
### Clarity, Conciseness, Diction, Emphasis

In this unit, students learn to control and vary their sentences through activities in *sentence combining*. Sentence combining, a practical outgrowth of linguistic analysis, requires that students transform lists of short *kernel* sentences into longer structures. The process teaches students to weigh ideas and to connect them in ways that indicate their relationships.

Here is a sample list for combination into a single sentence:

*The spider was ugly.*
*The spider was hairy.*
*The spider throbbed.*
*The spider threatened.*
*The spider was on the shelf.*
*The shelf was beside Pedro.*
*Pedro did not flinch.*

Students can combine these kernel sentences in several ways.

*The ugly, hairy spider throbbed and threatened on the shelf beside him, but Pedro did not flinch.*

*Although the spider, ugly and hairy, throbbed threateningly on the shelf beside him, Pedro did not flinch.*

*On the shelf beside Pedro throbbed and threatened an ugly, hairy spider that didn't make Pedro flinch.*

Other combinations are possible, too. A sense of the rich variety of English sentence structure results from sentence combining. In most cases, no single combination is "right"; different combinations present different implications and shades of meaning. Experimentation with and analysis of combinations increase the sophistication of students' understanding of language and also encourage flexibility of style.

A limitation of sentence combining is that students work with the ideas and the words of others rather than with their own. But it is an effective way to begin talking about the relationships among ideas, an efficient teacher of subordination and coordination, and a practice ground for learning how to achieve emphasis through sentence structure.

**Discussion.** Sentence combining allows students to put ideas together in a variety of ways. Some of these combinations communicate to an audience more clearly and economically than others, however. When they combine simple kernel sentences into larger sentences, and eventually into paragraphs, students should aim at the following:

- *Conciseness.* The kernel sentences contain redundancies, and students should make the wording more economical wherever they can.
- *Clarity.* The relationships among the ideas or details in the kernel sentences should be clear. The chief determiner of clarity is usually the combining word or phrase (often a subordinating or coordinating conjunction—*although, because, but*).
- *Diction.* When they can, students should replace dull or abstract words with more active and precise ones. They should look hard at nouns and verbs.
- *Emphasis.* If the ideas or details in the kernel sentences are equal in importance, the combination should be balanced, or coordinate, in structure; if they are unequal, students should generally place lesser ideas in phrases or subordinate clauses. Students should try to place key ideas in emphatic sentence patterns, such as contrast, repetition, and inverted order, within paragraphs.

**Preliminary Writing.** Put the following lists of kernel sentences on the board. Ask students to combine each list into a single, well-constructed sentence.

A *Susanna loves asparagus.*
 *She loves asparagus cooked until it is very tender.*
 *She can't stand spinach.*
 *She can't stand spinach in any form.*
B *Vandalism is on the rise at school.*
 *Now the senior class is determined to stop vandalism.*
C *Few hotel lobbies now have spittoons.*
 *Not many people chew tobacco anymore.*

D  *The chef had a big knife.*
   *The knife bit through the meat.*
   *The meat was red.*
   *The meat was juicy.*
   *The meat was succulent.*
   *The meat was a cut of beef.*

E  *A rock band makes a loud noise.*
   *The noise can be more than 90 decibels.*
   *Exposure to 90 decibels of noise can cause damage.*
   *The damage is to one's hearing.*
   *Rock music is popular.*
   *Its popularity is greater than ever.*

F  *His attention wanders.*
   *His eyes glaze.*
   *He hums to himself.*
   *He grins like a well-fed seal.*
   *He is in love.*

**Discussion.** Point out that no one combination is "right" or "wrong," that different combinations produce somewhat different meanings. Then ask five students—or more, if you have the space—to put their combinations on the board.

A common combination for list A is a balanced contrast structure that uses *but* as a coordinating conjunction:

*Susanna loves asparagus cooked until it is very tender, but she can't stand spinach in any form.*

Such a combination is appropriate to these ideas since the two parts (Susanna loves asparagus; Susanna can't stand spinach) are equal in importance. Other students combine the two ideas with a conjunctive adverb (*however*); this combination also preserves the contrast. Joining the two ideas with *and* suggests that the combiner perceives no contrast in ideas; ask if indeed he or she means that.

Some students combine without using a subject in the second part of the sentence ( . . . tender but can't stand . . . ). Such a combination is economical, but it is less emphatic than a balanced contrast.

List B can produce a variety of combinations. Again, some will be balanced, either contrasting or not:

*Vandalism is on the rise, but (or and) the senior class is determined to stop it.*

This combination implies that the rise of vandalism and the determination of the senior class to stop it are equally important.

The following examples give more emphasis to the senior class's determination to stop the vandalism.

> Although vandalism is on the rise at school, the senior class is determined to stop it.
>
> The senior class is determined to stop the vandalism that is on the rise at school.

On the other hand, if the increase in vandalism is the larger idea, a student might write:

> Although the senior class is determined to stop it, vandalism at school is on the rise.

Choice of the more important idea often depends on the *context*—on the sentences that precede and follow. Since in this preliminary activity those sentences are not available, selection of either idea is usually acceptable. Discuss the effect of different combinations.

When students put their versions of list C on the board, the class should see mostly sentences made up of one main clause and one subordinate clause, expressing a relationship of cause and effect:

> Since not many people chew tobacco anymore, few hotel lobbies have spittoons.

Is there a student who, working for better diction, has replaced *have* with a stronger verb (*feature, display*—but not *possess*) that adds prominence to that big brass object? Good. If not, ask students to find such a verb.

Most combinations of list D make the list into a concise, clear, accumulative simple sentence (just one clause):

> The chef's knife bit through the juicy red cut of beef.

Perhaps someone with a strong vocabulary has recognized that, since *succulent* and *juicy* are synonymous, the list contains a redundancy that a concise combination should eliminate. If no one has spotted the redundancy, point it out yourself. This is an opportunity to make a pitch for *clarity*. Ask the students which word, *succulent* or *juicy*, they would prefer to use, and discuss the merits of each. *Succulent* has a good sound to it, to be sure, but it is less direct than *juicy*. *Juicy* also has sound appeal; it is shorter;

most importantly, it communicates clearly to an audience. *Succulent*, a less familiar word, does not communicate—proof lies in the fact that most students will not recognize the redundancy.

Combinations of list E should produce a variety of different ways to subordinate. Although this list poses difficulties to some students who do not readily see how to combine the parts into a single sentence, if they study the relationships among the ideas, they should be able to create structures that express those relationships. The list also contains opportunities for *conciseness*.

Examine the various possibilities for combining list E. Note how certain students have eliminated words (like *noise*) for conciseness and how lesser ideas appear in subordinate clauses or phrases. Also consider the main idea. Which idea is it? Where is it placed in the sentence? Is it set in a main clause? Although most students suggest that the high popularity of rock music is the main idea, it needn't necessarily be so. And although the list suggests that high popularity comes at the end of the sentence, it needn't. The important thing is to choose a main idea and then give it prominent treatment.

In list F, details of equal importance are usually combined into parallel or balanced structure. The inference from or explanation of the details occurs at the end of the list; it generally occurs at the end of a combination, too, although variations are possible.

*His attention wanders; his eyes glaze; he hums to himself, grinning like a well-fed seal: he is in love.*

*If his attention wanders, his eyes glaze, he hums to himself, and he grins like a well-fed seal, you know he's in love.*

*Because he is in love, his attention wanders, and he hums to himself and grins like a well-fed seal.*

As you discuss the effects of various combinations, point out with examples that the most emphatic parts of a sentence are the beginning and the end. Then you can review lists A through F to demonstrate some of the many ways one can achieve sentence emphasis.

*Emphatic* sentences call attention to themselves; they insist that the ideas they contain are worthy of notice. Some of the sentences that students combined in the preliminary writing exercise lend themselves to emphatic combination. With reference to the specific patterns for emphasis exemplified on pages 21–24, here are some possible combinations:

COMBINING SENTENCES   53

DICTION.   (list E) Although the 90 decibel *thunder* of a rock band can damage one's hearing, rock music is more popular than ever.
FIGURE.   (list B) The senior class plans to clap a big manhole cover on the vandalism that is welling up from the sewer-dwelling element at school.
PLACEMENT.   (list C) Because not many people chew tobacco anymore, few hotel lobbies have spittoons.
ORDER.   (list D) Through the red, juicy, succulent cut of beef bit the chef's big knife.
REPETITION.   (list F) Attention wandering, eyes glazing, lips humming, he grins like a well-fed seal—he is in love.
CONTRAST.   (list A) Susanna loves asparagus cooked until it is very tender, but she cannot stand spinach in any form.

***Preliminary Writing.***   Here are 17 more lists for students to combine into single sentences. Some of the later lists present interesting complexities. As they combine, students should bear in mind the elements of *clarity, conciseness, diction,* and *emphasis.* When students are finished combining, analyze the combinations as you did lists A through F.

G   *Needlepoint is an old craft.*
    *Needlepoint is coming into vogue again.*
H   *You can legally operate a motorcycle.*
    *You must first pass a test.*
I   *The gymnast bounds into the air.*
    *He grasps the high bar.*
    *He swings in a fluid loop.*
J   *Nairobi is the capital of Kenya.*
    *It was rebuilt in the 1920s.*
    *It was rebuilt partly on a swamp.*
    *The swamp had been drained.*
K   *Maria is studying hydraulics.*
    *She plans to be a mechanical engineer.*
L   *The waters swirled.*
    *The waters burbled.*
    *The waters sucked the galleon down.*
    *The waters closed above the wreck.*
M   *The winner smiles expansively at the crowd.*
    *The crowd roars.*
    *The loser grimaces.*
    *The loser stalks off the platform.*

N  *Ben is my brother.*
   *He owns a motorcycle.*
   *It is a big Harley cycle.*
   *Ben keeps it in a tent.*

O  *Don likes to keep up with the latest dances.*
   *His sister Rita never dances at all.*

P  *More boys are babysitting these days.*
   *More girls are playing Little League baseball.*

Q  *Jan loves to play poker.*
   *Jan rarely wins at poker.*

R  *It was nighttime.*
   *A ring was around the moon.*
   *The sailors saw the ring.*
   *The sailors decided.*
   *Their decision was to sail in the morning anyway.*

S  *The World Series is being played.*
   *Many people don't usually watch baseball.*
   *People who don't usually watch baseball turn on their television sets.*

T  *Soybeans are grown in the United States.*
   *They are now a principal crop.*
   *They were grown 5,000 years ago.*
   *Then they were grown in China.*

U  *Millions of Americans have taken up jogging.*
   *Foot injuries have increased.*
   *"Sports medicine" clinics are jammed.*
   *The clinics are full of joggers.*

V  *Being in the sun can have two kinds of effects on our bodies.*
   *One kind of effect is good.*
   *One kind of effect is bad.*
   *Our bodies produce Vitamin D when sunlight strikes our skin.*
   *The sun can burn our skin.*
   *Years and years of exposure to the sun can cause skin cancers.*

W  *The defender flailed wildly.*
   *He used his arms and his hands.*
   *He jumped up and down.*
   *The player with the ball shot it.*
   *The ball swished through the basket.*

**Discussion.** This writing assignment has students combine longer lists of sentences to make paragraphs. In the sentences they combined earlier, students sought to achieve *emphasis* by appropriate subordination or coordination and by attention-getting structure. Achieving emphasis in paragraphs certainly implies appropriate placement of the most significant idea or detail. But remind students that stating that idea or detail in an interesting sentence structure is also important and is a goal of these activities.

**Prewriting.** Duplicate, or write on the board for students to copy, the lists of sentences in the writing assignment that follows. Ask students to indicate by drawing an arrow in the margin the most important idea or detail. Then students should underline potential problems in *clarity* and *diction*. Fuzzily structured sentences that appear difficult to combine challenge the student's ability to make clear combined sentences. Words that lack vigor and precision, especially abstract nouns, test the writer's ability to use strong diction. Effective combinations are strong in clarity and diction, as well as in syntax.

Students may change sentence order if they wish. They may also change nouns and verbs in favor of better diction.

**Writing.** Students are to combine the list of details in "Fast Lane" into a paragraph. Then they are to do the same for "Gridiron Gladiator" and "Two Points." As students write, they should work on *diction* (checking the list's word choice and improving it if possible), *clarity* (making clear links between simple sentences and testing for direct, accurate statements), and *conciseness* (eliminating redundant phrases and pruning wordy sentences). They should be sure that they highlight the most important detail in an emphatic sentence. Encourage originality—within the bounds of clear, economical communication.

*FAST LANE*
1. *A car pulled out.*
2. *The car was long.*
3. *The car was black.*
4. *It was a limousine.*
5. *It went onto the freeway.*
6. *It accelerated rapidly.*
7. *It swung out.*
8. *It went into the middle lane.*
9. *Then it went into the fast lane.*
10. *It passed every car.*
11. *It flashed its lights.*
12. *The flashing was at other cars.*
13. *The other cars were slow to get out of its way.*

## GRIDIRON GLADIATOR

1. He is helmeted.
2. His shoulders are thickly padded.
3. His thighs bulge.
4. His calves bulge.
5. He is clad in green.
6. The football player emerges.
7. He comes from the tunnel.
8. The tunnel comes from the dressing room.
9. There is a roar.
10. The roar is from the crowd.
11. The crowd is large.
12. The crowd is passionate.
13. The crowd is eager for victory.
14. The air is charged.
15. The air is emotional.
16. The player is oblivious.
17. He does not hear the cheers.
18. He does not notice the stands.
19. The stands are teeming.
20. He thinks only of the job.
21. He must do the job today.
22. The whistle blows.
23. The player trots onto the field.
24. He is determined.
25. The determination is to "knock some heads."

## TWO POINTS

1. The wastebasket stands tall.
2. The wastebasket is in the hallway.
3. The wastebasket is silent.
4. The wastebasket waits.
5. A bell rings.
6. Doors fly open.
7. Students jostle.
8. They are leaving classrooms.
9. Some of the students are muttering.
10. They are muttering about a test.
11. The test was in math.
12. The test was hard.
13. The test was just returned.
14. The students crumple paper.
15. The crumpled paper is in the shape of little balls.
16. The students hurl the balls.

17. Their goal is the wastebasket.
18. The balls go into the wastebasket.
19. One student hollers.
20. "Two points!" is what he says.

## Marking Guidelines

* *Diction.* Has the writer found precise, active words to insert in place of dull diction? (Look at sentences 10-13 of "Fast Lane" and 10-14 of "Gridiron Gladiator" to see what verbs students have found.)
* *Clarity.* Are the ideas clear? Are the transitions between ideas accurate? (Look especially at subordinating conjunctions and at participles.)
* *Conciseness.* Has the writer eliminated the many redundancies in the lists? Has he or she condensed the phrasing? (Look at 17-22 of "Gridiron Gladiator.")
* *Emphasis.* In "Fast Lane," the most emphatic spot is either the beginning or the end; in the other two combinations, the most important idea occurs at the end of the list. Has the student expressed that idea in a sentence that gets the attention of the audience without awkwardness?

## Sample Combinations

### FAST LANE

A long black limousine pulled out onto the freeway. Accelerating rapidly, it swung out into the middle lane, then into the fast lane. It passed every other car, flashing its lights at cars that were slow to move out of the way.

### GRIDIRON GLADIATOR

Helmeted, shoulders thickly padded, thighs and calves bulging, the green-clad football player bursts out of the tunnel from the dressing room. A roar erupts from the huge crowd passionate for victory. The air is charged with emotion. But the player is oblivious to the cheers from the teeming stands; he thinks only of the job he must do today. As the whistle blows, the player charges onto the field, determined to "knock some heads."

### TWO POINTS

The wastebasket waits, tall and silent in the hallway. As a bell rings, doors fly open and students emerge jostling one another. Muttering about a hard math test that has just been returned, the *students approach the wastebasket, crumpling papers into balls. They hurl the paper balls at the wastebasket. As his ball lands in the wastebasket, one student hollers, "Two points!"*

**Comments.** Whereas the first combination is conservative, preserving the order of ideas and the diction of the original, the other two combinations take some liberties in order to achieve clarity and emphasis. All three are concise.

# UNIT TWO
# BUILDING PARAGRAPHS

## ELEMENTS OF GOOD WRITING
### Coherence, Emphasis, Unity

In this unit, we move from the sentence to the paragraph. A sentence states a single thought; a paragraph is the development of that single thought. It may be considered a unit of thought, a building block for the composition.

How long should a paragraph be? Well, the paragraph is really a convenience to the reader; it aids accurate and comfortable communication. Therefore a paragraph should not be so short as to supply inadequate or unintentionally puzzling treatment of an idea; nor should it be so long as to bore the reader. The modern tendency, shaped by our electronic age, is toward short paragraphs. Still, an unbroken succession of staccato paragraphs can bore a reader just as several long ones can. Variety in length is important: a long paragraph to develop background information, a short one to give emphasis to a key point. Although there are certain guidelines for forming paragraphs, there is no set formula to follow; it is a matter of taste and style.

For these activities, you will need many examples of paragraphs that vary in subject matter, style, length, and date of composition. You can find these examples in a textbook that your students already have, or you can compile and duplicate your own collection of examples. In any case, seek examples of quality. Also, try to find paragraphs on subjects that will interest your students. Find at least 10 paragraphs.

**Preliminary Writing.** Before the students begin to write, have them do some analysis to create awareness of the objectives of unity, coherence, and emphasis. Choose six paragraphs—some with obvious topic sentences, some without. As you present them to the class (duplicated or written on the board), save until the end those paragraphs in which the central idea is difficult to recognize.

Tell the students to underline the topic sentence, if there is one, in each paragraph. Also have them write the central idea of each paragraph—whether or not it is expressed in a topic sentence—in their own words.

Next have the class scan each paragraph for transitions and circle them. Finally, indicate with an arrow in the margin where students think the *emphasis* falls in each paragraph.

**Discussion.** Review with the class the concepts of *unity*, *coherence*, and *emphasis*, pointing out the variety of ways these are achieved in the six paragraphs.

A paragraph achieves its *unity* as it grows outward, free of irrelevancies, from a single central idea. The central idea is often stated in a topic sentence, and the topic sentence often occurs at the beginning of the paragraph. Not always, though. Many paragraphs do not have topic sentences; however, if they are well-unified paragraphs, a reader may infer the central idea and state it in his or her own words, as in the preceding activity. For reasons of emphasis, a topic sentence may come at the end of a paragraph, or even in the middle, rather than at the beginning. If there is no central idea at all, the paragraph is wobbly, and lacking in unity.

Paragraph *coherence* comes from a logical ordering of ideas (for example, least to most important, first to last) and from an effective use of transitional words and phrases (*next, on the other hand, furthermore*, and so on).

*Emphasis*, the third determiner of an effective paragraph, is chiefly the result of the placement of the central idea. The easiest way to achieve emphasis is to place the central idea in a topic sentence at the start of the paragraph and develop the idea deductively. However, more striking emphasis often results when the central idea comes at the end. The key idea might not be stated in a topic sentence at all—perhaps in just a vibrant word or phrase. In any case, paragraph emphasis is enhanced if the key idea is not only well placed but also set in a sentence that is itself emphatic.

**Writing.** As the writing assignment for this unit, each student is to write six paragraphs. Two are to be written in class, four for homework.

To simplify the three-part emphasis in these activities and to let ideas sink in a bit, divide the activities into two parts. For the first, assign one paragraph in class and two for homework. When you analyze the papers, focus more on unity and coherence than on emphasis.

Let a day or two pass after you have analyzed and returned the papers. Then assign another paragraph in class and two more for homework. This time work on emphasis, although it is important also to reinforce unity and coherence.

You should assign topics for the paragraphs. There are two criteria for the topics: they should be familiar to the students (no research necessary), and they should be narrow enough for appropriate treatment in a single paragraph. The topics might come from literature, or from school life, or from your town; or they might be of a more general nature. Make a list of topics. Here is a sample list:
- ◇ the significance of the pearl in Steinbeck's story "The Pearl"
- ◇ one use for the bulletin board
- ◇ where the bus goes
- ◇ what a mouse will eat
- ◇ the best stride for distance running
- ◇ when to change a car's oil
- ◇ a mushroom you can eat
- ◇ the knuckle ball

Allow the students 3 minutes to choose their topics. Give them 15 minutes to write a paragraph, but do not give any other directions or answer questions.

**Discussion.** After 15 minutes, have students exchange paragraphs, and ask them to find the topic sentence, state the central idea in their own words, circle transitions, and indicate emphasis as they did in the Preliminary Writing exercise. Have students return each other's papers.

As students review their classmates' analyses, point out that well-built paragraphs analyze well. Those that sprawl or wander, or that contain irrelevant details, do not. Also point out that a paragraph is a developed single thought.

After students have written and analyzed their in-class paragraphs, assign two more paragraphs for homework. Assign topics, or let students choose from a short list, so that they do not have to cast about for ideas before they can begin to write. When the papers come in, have students exchange them again and analyze one of the paragraphs as before. Let each student see his or her own paper after it has been analyzed by another. Then collect the papers to analyze the second paragraphs yourself.

After a day or so, repeat the process: paragraph in class, analysis; two paragraphs for homework, analysis. This time focus on emphasis. When students analyze the papers, have them indicate with an arrow the emphasis of the paragraph: Is it in the topic sentence or elsewhere? If elsewhere, how is it achieved?

**Marking Guidelines.** It is not necessary to mark all of the paragraphs. Mark the second one done in class, and one or two of those written for homework.

* *Unity.* Is the central idea clear? Are there any extraneous details?
* *Coherence.* Do ideas flow in a sensible order? Are transitions effective?
* *Emphasis.* In most student paragraphs, emphasis occurs in a beginning topic sentence. However, some students may try for more subtle effects. If the paragraph is unified and coherent, and the student has placed the most striking idea elsewhere than in an obvious topic sentence, good!

## Sample Paragraphs

A  *Acting on a stage may seem to be very simple: stand up and pretend you are someone else. However, there is much more to it than that. First of all, the actor must concentrate on his voice. Is it loud and clear enough? Does it contain a good range of emotions, varying levels of volume, and good timing with correct pauses? Secondly, the face of the actor and its series of expressions is half the portrayal of his character. Do the facial emotions correspond with the voice intonations? They should. Finally, the body language and movement of an actor play an important role in convincing the audience of the character. Voice, facial expressions, and movement are three key factors in acting.*

—ROBIN HARUTUNIAN

B  *There is some force within human nature that attracts us all to the roller coaster. Perhaps it is the challenge of surviving the machine. You anxiously hop in and climb toward the sky. The apex of the ascent is followed by a gentle U-turn, where you sense the almost frictionless contact between the metal wheels and track. Then the car dips, apparently straight down, as you experience weightlessness. Predictably you head back up, but this series of left and right turns confuses the path of your journey. You jolt to a stop with a blur of memories.*

—RALPH HARTMANN

**Comments.** Both of these are strong paragraphs. Paragraph A achieves something rare in student work: inductive development to a closing topic sentence. The second sentence states the thesis, but development is not full until the end—difficult emphasis, but successful. The paragraph is unified; all details bear on the central idea that acting is a difficult art which demands three kinds of expertise. The paragraph is rich in transitions ("However," "First of all," "Secondly") and gains further in coherence from the question-answer structure.

Paragraph B is a colorful description of a roller coaster ride. The first sentence is in a sense misleading, but it is a strong lead-in to the paragraph. Although there is no topic sentence, the central idea is clear and the paragraph contains no extraneous details. The writer achieves coherence cleverly by following the course of the ride itself.

# UNIT THREE
# ILLUSTRATING A SCENE

### ELEMENTS OF GOOD WRITING
### Clarity, Coherence, Diction, Emphasis

These activities draw on your students' ability to observe; they emphasize description that is at once accurate and imaginative. The writing assignments demand that students employ tight, consistent structure. Students learn that the organizational principles that we urge in their writing have counterparts in the real world. The job of the writer, like that of the observer, is to make sense of what is out there and then to convey it to an audience in a clear, economical manner.

The vehicle for this set of activities is a natural scene. The setting of the scene does not matter. It may be found inside or outside the classroom. Since going outside provides a change of pace and more stimulating subject matter, go outside if you can.

Students are to choose segments of the scene in front of them and describe them briefly. At first, let them describe the scene spontaneously. Eventually, you should be able to bring them to understand that in order to communicate well to their audience, they must organize carefully.

***Preliminary Writing.*** Each student is to select a 60-degree arc of view. Indicate some sample arcs by spreading your arms. Tell the students to describe the view that they have chosen in a paragraph or two. They should try to interest their readers in the descriptions, and the readers should be able to picture the views in their own minds when they read the descriptions. Allow 30 minutes for writing.

***Discussion.*** After 30 minutes, students are to exchange papers. Each reader tries to indicate, by spreading arms, the arc of view described in the paper. Point out that discrepancies, confusion, and misunderstanding are likely the fault of the writer, not the reader. Precision and organization characterize the papers that communicate effectively.

Collect the papers and read several aloud to the class (the next class period is fine for this). As you review the papers with the students, discuss how the papers have or have not conveyed an accurate picture of what is being described.

Coherence in the composition depends mostly on two things—structure and transitions. A well-structured paper describes objects according to a consistent pattern: near to far, left to right, upper right to lower left, straight along a path or street or wall, and so forth. Try to find any such organizational schemes in the student papers and praise them, even if those schemes are not maintained consistently throughout the paragraphs. Point out that, just as we can discern an order of objects in the real world, so, too, should we order ideas in our writing.

Transitions in these papers will mostly be "space" words: "on the right," "further along," "just above," "five feet to the left." These help the mind's eye to follow the pen's journey. "Time" words, like "next" and "then," are thus out of place in a spatial description.

Point out some descriptions in which relative locations of objects are easy to follow and some in which a reader becomes lost. *Clarity* is related to coherence in this activity, in that if we cannot see where we are because of unclear description, it is hard to know where we have been or where we are going.

In addition to using accurate words (which are another component of clarity in the activity), students should look for brisk and vivid nouns and adjectives. "A church" is vague; "a dusty brick church" becomes clearer through more imaginative *diction*. Verbs can stand scrutiny, too. Sentences using "there is a . . . " (expletive construction) are far less interesting than those in which verbal pep is supplied by words like "leans" or "pokes out."

Where does the description lead? Does it just trickle out, or does it feature a memorable detail, like a beckoning attic window or a lonely old man? *Emphasis* in this sort of description is likely achieved in a detail that occurs at the end, but it might occur in the middle (details leading up to it, then away) or at the beginning (details receding into the distance).

**Prewriting.** It may help your class to see one or two examples of clearly structured description. Here is one from John Ruskin's *The Stones of Venice*. It is just one sentence long—but what a sentence! The class should easily be able to discern the structural scheme: the writer takes his readers on a walking tour of a street, at the end of which lies a cathedral.

*Let us go together up the more retired street, at the end of which we can see the pinnacles of one of the towers, and then through the low, grey gateway with its battlemented top and small latticed window in the center, into the inner private-looking road or close, where nothing goes in but the carts of the tradesmen who supply the bishop and the chapter, and here there are little shaven grassplots, fenced in by neat rails, before old-fashioned groups of somewhat diminutive and excessively trimmed houses, with little oriel and bay windows jutting out here and there, and deep wooden cornices and eaves painted cream colour and white, and small porches to their doors in the shape of cockleshells, or little, crooked, thick, indescribable, wooden gables warped a little on one side; and so forward till we come to the larger houses, also old-fashioned, but of red brick, and with gardens behind them, and fruit walls, which show here and there, among the nectarines, the vestiges of an old cloister arch or shaft; and looking in front on the cathedral square itself, laid out in rigid divisions of smooth grass and gravel walk, yet not uncheerful, especially on the sunny side, where the canons' children are walking with their nurserymaids.*[22]

If you can, draw examples of spatial description from the books your class is reading now. A fine twentieth-century word-picture of this sort is F. Scott Fitzgerald's first description of the Buchanans' house in *The Great Gatsby*.

For homework, students rewrite their word-pictures. This time they must use some structural pattern like those suggested on page 65.

**Discussion.** In class the next day, have students exchange papers. Ask each reader to identify and describe at the bottom of the paper the plan of organization that he or she sees at work in the paper. Readers should circle all transitional words and phrases. Then they should look for details, marking with exclamation points those details that they find fresh and interesting and indicating with horizontal arrows details that they believe are out of order. Finally, the readers should write a brief assessment of the clarity and quality of the word-picture. Included in their comments should be mention of the degree of improvement from the original effort in class.

**Writing.** Students choose their own scenes for this assignment. In a one-page composition, they describe a scene chosen according to certain guidelines. The scene—

◇ may be indoors or outdoors
◇ must contain plenty of space and depth of field (it should not be cramped or two-dimensional)
◇ should be rich in objects, though not overcrowded
◇ must interest the writer

## Marking Guidelines

❖ *Coherence.*   Is there an effective and consistent organizational structure? Are transitions adequate and clear? Are all details in logical order?

❖ *Clarity.*   Are directions and locations readily comprehensible? Can you actually picture the arc of view? If not, why not?

❖ *Diction.*   Does the composition employ vivid, precise, concrete words? Are the verbs colorful?

❖ *Emphasis.*   Is there a clear focal point—an important image that the other details support? Does this central image receive emphatic placement within the scheme of organization?

## Sample Description

*A cold, unfriendly wind gusts under the leaden sky, rustling the leaves in the trees and sending those that have already fallen scudding over the grass. Directly to my right begins the great sprawl of the gym complex. This part of it has a Georgian look to it: reddish-brown brick, tall arched windows, and a tiled roof rising symmetrically towards a rounded cupola topped by a weather vane. A bright blue Athletic Department minibus in front of the building sets a rather odd tone in an otherwise old world scene. Moving down the building, however, there is a sudden, startling change. Functional American architecture at its best (or worst) takes over, combining with the older style in a rather revolting manner. Now the accent is on steel and glass. There is still brick, but it has none of the warm glow of the older style. When the sky clears for a moment and a ray of sunshine strikes through, the new brick remains cold, perfect, and institutional.*

*Moving down the line we come to the sheet metal expanse of the hockey rink, with the roof of the cage rising in the background. The color of the metal is by turns dull grey and then bright silver as the sun shines on it.*

*Past the hockey rink we leave modernization and efficiency behind at last and come to greener things: the dark green of the hedge-encircled varsity tennis courts; the lighter green, fading now toward autumn brown, of the athletic fields, and the green of a massive oak tree rising in the distance. All of this is partially obscured by a screen of golden leaves cast by a large maple in front of me.*

*The wind picks up again; leaves blow in my face. It is time to go.*
—RICHARD MURPHY

**Comments.** Coherence in the piece is produced by a number of spatial transitions and by a scheme of details that are ordered from near to far and from up to down at the same time. Note, however, that one details jars: that blue minibus might be perched atop a weather vane! Most of the details are clear, although at times more concrete information is lacking ("the roof of the cage" needs clarification, for instance). Diction is sharp and clear. However, the writer lapses at times into unemphatic syntax ("There is still brick, but it has none . . . " in paragraph one). The introduction of the writer's bias against modern architecture is both a weakness and a strength. It risks alienating the audience, but it sets up the point of emphasis of the description—the natural greenery—toward which the piece works. A final point: the description gains unity and interest from the use of a *frame*. The writer begins and ends with the wind, a detail that involves both him and his audience in the description.

UNIT FOUR
# NARRATING A JOURNEY

### ELEMENTS OF GOOD WRITING
Active Voice, Development, Diction, Emphasis, Originality

For this unit, students take a journey. They may travel by automobile, subway, bus, bicycle, foot—any means will do. The journey should last between 15 and 30 minutes. If it is a portion of a longer trip, the starting and ending points of the portion should be clear.

During their journeys students are merely to observe what they see, what goes on around them, and what happens to them. Immediately at the end of the journey, they are to make notes on what they have observed.

From their notes they are to select one observation or incident that they will treat as the highlight of the trip. This observation or incident is to be the focal point of the narrative account of the journey that they will write.

**Discussion.** Discuss the concept of *emphasis* in writing. Sometimes the focal point, or place of greatest emphasis, of a paragraph or a longer piece occurs in the middle of the piece, but most often it occurs at the beginning or the end. It takes great subtlety and control to create successful emphasis in the middle; therefore, learning writers would do best to place emphasis at the start of their papers.

A news story is a common example of initial emphasis. You can use several stories from newspapers and magazines to show how the writer has put the most important (or most interesting in a feature story) detail at the start of the article and then used other details to support that initial detail.

**Preliminary Writing.** Have students name some important events that have happened in the world, in their town or city, or at school during the last week. Then write, or ask a student to write, these events on the board in the form of newspaper headlines. Examples:
- ◊ Warriors Defeat Newbold
- ◊ President to Visit China
- ◊ Bill Caster Elected to Student Council
- ◊ Air Hijacker Captured

Students are to choose a topic from the list and write a news story about it for homework. They may take details from personal experience or from the visual or print media. If they use material from television or newspapers, they must identify their sources and use quotations where appropriate.

**_Discussion._** When the papers come in, have students exchange them. Tell readers to mark the most important idea, the focal point in the story, with a large arrow in the margin. The arrow should point to the beginning of the story. After papers have been returned, collect them and read a few aloud, pausing to comment on effective leads.

The set of news stories should provide examples of misuse of the passive voice. A newspaper editor will tell reporters that names make news and that their leads should be vigorous. Those two concepts dictate (in most cases) the use of the *active voice*. If a student has written "A meeting of the Senior Advisory Council was held . . . ," you can show how much more informative and interesting the lead would be if it began "At a meeting of the Senior Advisory Council, . . . " and went on to mention the highlight of the meeting. Even if nothing happened in the meeting, a better lead than the first one would be, "Thirteen members of the Senior Advisory Council met . . . " since it conveys more information and is actively cast.

Put both passive and active leads on the board and compare them for clarity, conciseness, vigor, and information value. Then ask students to rewrite some of the passive leads in the active voice.

In much fiction, unlike newspaper writing, emphasis falls at the end, in a climax. The cartoons that children watch on television provide obvious examples of end emphasis. Episodes, each with its climax, increase in intensity until they reach a final catastrophe for the villain. Narratives also often rely on end emphasis, as the account builds up to a significant event. In this paragraph from Amelia Earhart's *Last Flight*, end emphasis occurs; the structure of this piece of narrative exposition is chronological.

*At 3:45 A.M. we were warming up the engines at Bandoeng, planning, if all went well, to fly through to Australia. When one instrument refused to function everyone present turned mechanic and set to work to help. But it was not until two o'clock in the afternoon that the distemper was sufficiently cured to warrant proceeding. After that late start we reached Saurabaya when the descending sun marked declining day. In the air, and afterward, we found that our mechanical troubles had not been cured. Certain further adjustments of faulty long-distance flying instruments were necessary, and so I had to do one of the most difficult things I had ever done in aviation. Instead of keeping on I turned back the next day to Bandoeng.*[23]

Emphasize that interesting narratives contain a variety of details. Readers will not likely enjoy a narrative that contains only a list of landmarks, or only a running description of the observer's feelings, or only details about the weather. A mixture of details is best. And writers can mix those details coherently by finding connections between them (between a sunny spring day and the good feeling of the observer, for instance; or between a block of tall buildings and the shade they cast) and by using appropriate transitions, particularly time and space ("then," "two minutes later," "on the next corner").

Variety in sentence structure is also important. It is tedious to read a succession of sentences that begin "Next I saw . . . " or "There were. . . . "

**Preliminary Writing.** Assign a narrative paragraph for homework. Students should describe something they did or something that happened to them in the past two days. As in the Earhart paragraph, emphasis should fall at the end of the student paragraph. The paragraph should consist of a variety of details arranged chronologically, leading up to the most important part of the event.

**Discussion.** As with the news stories, have students exchange papers, examine emphasis, and consider leads and active voice. Have students count the different details and then the different kinds of details: buildings, people, actions, colors, sounds, smells, weather. Collect papers and pick out some effective transitions to read to the class.

**Prewriting.** Ask for precise details about a journey someone in the class has taken. Draw out as many details as you can. Where did the traveler start? What did the scene at the beginning look like? How did the traveler proceed along the journey? What objects did he or she notice along the way? What sights were most interesting? Most important? Why? What was the destination? What did the traveler see there first?

It will probably seem more natural to your students to begin their narratives at the beginning and end at the end rather than to fiddle around with details and emphasis. However, it is likely that the most significant part of the trip was not the beginning or end, but somewhere in the middle. And, for the sake of this assignment, you should *require* that students choose as their focal point a significant detail from the middle, so that they will have to wrestle with emphasis and organizational problems.

That significant detail must then be placed in an emphatic position: either near the beginning or near the end. This sort of placement will require expansion of the focal detail and condensation of other details.

Early placement of emphasis requires the writer to present most previous details through flashbacks. Perhaps the class has read a novel or short story that begins this way (a strong, compelling opening detail, followed by flashbacks to the events leading up to that detail or event); if so, it makes a good model for this sort of structure.

End focus is easier to achieve if the focal detail actually occurred near the end of the journey. No flashbacks, with their problems of clear, consistent verb tense, are required. But a writer who accepts the challenge of initial focus may gain more from the exercise than one who doesn't.

Students should list details before they begin to write. Lists should take form A for initial focus or form B for end focus.

| A | B |
|---|---|
| Detail 1 (on journey, immediately preceded focal detail) | Detail 1 (first detail on journey or introduction) |
| FOCAL DETAIL (detail 2) | Detail 2 (chronologically followed detail 1) |
| Flashback detail *a* (first detail on journey) | Detail 3 |
| Flashback detail *b* | Detail 4 |
| Flashback detail *c* | Detail 5 |
| Flashback detail *d* | Buildup for focal detail |
| Detail 3 (immediately followed focal detail) | FOCAL DETAIL |
| Detail 4 | Detail 6 |
| Detail 5 | |

You might wish to require more or fewer details or make focus even sharper by eliminating detail 1 in A and detail 6 in B. The structures are flexible.

**Writing.** The narration should be two pages long. This length necessitates *full development*. In this assignment, point out that development means both that the paper must contain a number of details sufficient to communicate the journey to the audience and that each detail must receive sufficient development to ensure that the audience grasps it. The significant detail that receives emphasis requires expansion and especially precise treatment.

Remind the class that narrative descriptions are memorable when their details are original. *Originality* depends on selection (what details freshly and economically capture the scene) and on presentation (how can the writer use this detail to involve the audience). Good selection requires ingenuity and avoidance of the commonplace; good presentation demands strong, clear *diction*, as well as some imagination. Compare:

> The power plant, with its tall smokestacks, was on my right.
>
> The stacks of the power house fume and sigh...
> —THOMAS MCGRATH

The diction and sentence structure of the second example give it emphasis and welcome originality.

**Discussion.** When the papers come in, ask several students to read their work aloud to the class. Ask the class to comment on the development of some of the details. Can they share the experience that the writer was trying to communicate? Ask the class where the focus lies in each paper. If the narratives become fuzzy to the class, look for the transitions the writer has used. Are they there? Are they clear?

As they edit and then revise their papers, students should concentrate on making the emphasis clear and strong and on improving diction by finding precise, vivid verbs and nouns.

## Marking Guidelines

❖ *Active voice.* Is the narrative dominated by strong, active constructions, rather than by passive and expletive constructions?

❖ *Development.* Are details sufficient in number? Are details, especially the most significant detail, fully described?

- *Diction.* Is the word choice concrete rather than abstract? Are the words appropriate? Has the writer made any exceptionally striking word choices?
- *Emphasis.* Where does the emphasis lie? Is it clear? Is a reader convinced that the emphasized detail is the most important detail in the narrative? Does the writer lead coherently into and away from the chief detail?
- *Originality.* Has the writer used a variety of details? Does the sentence structure vary for interest and emphasis? Are the details fresh and strikingly presented?

## Sample Narrative

*Solitary and journeying down a muddy dirt road marred with tire tracks, the sun beaming in my eyes, I felt miles away from the hubbub of daily academic life. On my right was a fairly dense woods chock-full of fallen limbs and trunks of trees, and on my left was a large and rustic fenced off garden full of doubled over, dried cornstalks. Huge black crows flew off "yalking" as I approached. The sunflowers hang their heads in despair because of the coming of winter. Unripe, green pumpkins, painfully contorted squash, and tomatoes squelched on the solid ground attest to how rich the harvest must have been. All is brown and dormant except for the herbs and grass. Repose is creeping through veins of the huge heads of wilting cabbage, the agrestic daisies, and the raspberry bushes which still have some red berries on them. I never before realized that mud has a distinct odor.*

*I rejoined the road heading due west, and every step I took produced a rattling sound as the pebbles knocked against each other. From time to time the tire tracks in the road disappeared, but there was always a vestige of man—the road itself, a newspaper tangled in the brush by the side of the road, and those plastic rings that hold six-packs together.*

*I experienced the feeling of aloneness, and yet Isham was still in view and the music it was emitting could still be heard. The rustling of the uncultivated plants and the "cheeps" coming from all sides reminded me that there was life nearby.*

*As I approached a fork in the road, I quickly decided that I should go to the right because that was the way that the tire tracks, now deep in the mud, went. The soil had eroded from the road, enough to expose a pipe that crosses it diagonally. As I continued along the road towards a destination still unknown, the road became yellow from the covering of dead grass that crackles underfoot.*

*The breeze picked up so that it was refreshing, but not chilling. The sun invited me to continue on my journey. A huge wall of dirt* on my left side is evidence of bulldozing. I heard the scratchy sound of crickets fiddling.

I reached my destination . . . alone. It is not exotic. It is not distant. This place is only where they dump the leaves that they remove from the rest of the campus. I had imagined coming across a log cabin, or a farm, or a hermit's cave, but these piles of decomposing leaves turned out to be the pot of gold at the end of my rainbow journey. All of the leaves are brown, not the beautifully brilliant oranges and reds that we see around the campus. These leaves are brown and dead in every sense of the word. Budweiser cans are visible through the leaves. Three cross sections of what must have been a domineering tree lie on the left edge of this clearing. A discarded black pail oozes black scum. The odor in this area is putrid. In the background is a beautiful living woods. I turned around to return to reality. The minute that I heard a car horn, I too again became part of the chaos.

—KAREN YASHAR

**Comments.** Strong and varied sentence constructions make this piece vivid. The writer has used only one expletive construction and one passive, neither obtrusively. She has supported abstractions with details and has described those details closely ("Repose is creeping through veins of . . . cabbage," "a newspaper tangled in the brush"). Some of the diction is striking—"contorted squash," "black pail oozes black scum"—although verbs in a few sentences are dull.

Emphasis, which is placed in the last paragraph, is clear because of the richness and amount of detail there, and also because of the emphatic sentences (repetition in sentences two and three is notable) that begin the paragraph. Originality in the narrative comes from the choice of different kinds of details. The irony of the "pot of gold" turning out to be decay and detritus is memorable, as is the reversal at the very end. Treatment of the entire narrative is fresh.

A teacher marking this piece should also, of course, point out the inconsistency of verb tense that runs through the paper.

UNIT FIVE
# SETTING A MOOD

### ELEMENTS OF GOOD WRITING
### Diction, Originality, Unity

Narrative and descriptive writing form the center of this unit in which students exercise imagination and originality while they carefully work with ideas and words toward a certain goal. For the writing activity, each student will select three ingredients—a character, a situation or event, and a mood—and work with them to produce a unified effect on the audience. Students should come to understand *tone* in writing through the study and use of two of its components, *mood* and *diction*.

***Discussion.*** A good way to lead into a discussion of mood, if the term is new to the class, is to focus on some fiction that students have recently read or are reading now. The excerpts in the discussion come from classics, but modern fiction is rich in useful pieces as well.

In addition to making students familiar with the concept of mood, the following preliminary discussion should bear fruit later on, when they will need to find people and events in the world around them that will help the development of their mood pieces.

Talk about moods that affect people. Ask someone what his or her mood is right now. What is the range of moods that members of the class have felt during the last 24 hours? The last week? Ask students to name objects, scenes, or events in the world around them that correspond to or reinforce their moods.

Mood in writing is much like mood as the class has been using the term. It is the emotional environment of a piece of writing. The mood of a poem, for instance, might be reflective (Wordsworth's "Tintern Abbey"), mystical (Coleridge's "Kubla Khan"), or sentimental (Whitman's "O Captain! My Captain!"). It might be somber, bitter, gleeful, foreboding, angry, cheerful—or it might be composed of several emotions.

How does a writer achieve a given mood? By choice of evocative details. From all of the tangible, sensual, and emotional parts that make up a scene or a moment, the writer selects those particular details that, when set down in an orderly way, will create for the reader the intended mood.

Here is a famous example of the creation of mood through the selection of details. In this passage from chapter 2 of *Bleak House*, Charles Dickens builds an overpowering mood of dampness, stagnation, and decay.

> The waters are out in Lincolnshire. An arch of the bridge in the park has been sapped and sopped away. The adjacent low-lying ground, for half a mile in breadth, is a stagnant river, with melancholy trees for islands in it, and a surface punctured all over, all day long, with falling rain. My lady Dedlock's "place" has been extremely dreary. The weather, for many a day and night, has been so wet that the trees seem wet through, and the soft loppings and prunings of the woodsman's axe can make no crack or crackle as they fall. The deer, looking soaked, leave quagmires where they pass. The shot of a rifle loses its sharpness in the moist air, and its smoke moves in a tardy little cloud towards the green rise, coppice-topped, that makes a background for the falling rain. The view from my Lady Dedlock's own windows is alternately a lead-coloured view, and a view in Indian ink. The vases on the stone terrace in the foreground catch the rain all day; and the heavy drops fall, drip, drip, drip, upon the broad flagged pavement, called, from old time, the Ghost's Walk, all night. On Sundays, the little church in the park is mouldy; the oaken pulpit breaks out into a cold sweat; and there is a general smell and taste as of the ancient Dedlocks in their graves.[24]

**Preliminary Writing.** In order to demonstrate how mood depends on diction, have students underline details from the preceding passage that contribute to the mood. Then have them change some of those details to dilute, change, or banish the mood altogether ("sapped and sopped away" could become "eroded"; "stagnant" could become "unmoving"; "melancholy trees" could become "bent-over trees"; and so forth). Have students finish the task for homework.

**Discussion.** Compare the revisions in class. Is there mood in the student versions? Is it the same mood as in Dickens's? What particular details establish mood? Although some students will have replaced evocative words with neutral synonyms, others will have established new moods. Emphasize that changes in diction change mood.

**Prewriting.** Ask each student to create a character. This character may be based on the student or on another real person, but should be made fictional by changes, at least in name. Have several students describe their characters briefly.

Here is a good place to talk about *originality*. Discuss the uniqueness of the characters described. Are they forgettable or unforgettable? What makes them so? What sorts of details make a strong impression? Have we met these characters before? What is wrong with stereotypical or stock characters?

Next, each character is to be set in a situation or event. Something is going on: perhaps something gentle and natural, like a snowfall; or something violent and of human origin, like a battle; or something in between these extremes—a visit to a toothpick factory, for instance. The combination of character and situation should produce a *unified* mood. The mood felt by the character in a snowfall might be peace or softness; that of a character in a pitched battle might be terror or savage joy.

Students should work together in small groups to present and clarify their characters, situations, and moods. Each student should have at least one opportunity to speak to the small group as if he or she were actually the fictional character, describing in the first person the situation in which that character has been placed. This helps students to find appropriate diction and to practice building mood through details; feedback from the group provides guidance and reinforcement.

If there is enough time, an enjoyable and useful activity is a conversation among members of the group, each speaking in the voice of the character he or she has created. Although such conversations are sometimes incoherent because each character is thinking of a different situation, they help to overcome shyness and to make the characters more familiar to their creators.

**Writing.** The writing assignment is to invent and select details about the situation and event that produce a consistent mood in the created character. The mood is conveyed to the reader through a first-person narrative by the character.

If you feel a concrete model would be helpful, you can show the class how Edgar Allen Poe uses the first person to set a mood in "The Fall of the House of Usher."

> *I know not how it was—but, with the first glimpse of the building, a sense of insufferable gloom pervaded my spirit. I say insufferable;*

> for the feeling was unrelieved by any of that half-pleasurable, because poetic, sentiment, with which the mind usually receives even the sternest natural images of the desolate or terrible. I looked upon the scene before me—upon the mere house, and the simple landscape features of the domain, upon the bleak walls, upon the vacant eye-like windows, upon a few rank sedges, and upon a few white trunks of decayed trees—with an utter depression of soul which I can compare to no earthly sensation more properly than to the after-dream of the reveler upon opium: the bitter lapse into every-day life, the hideous dropping off of the veil.[25]

The class can analyze this passage as they did the excerpt from *Bleak House*.

The *lead*, or opening sentence, is the key to the establishment of *unity* of mood. A lead may establish a character, as Melville's simple "Call me Ishmael" at the start of *Moby Dick* indicates a blunt man and a familiar relationship between speaker and audience. Or it can begin right away to establish mood, as Dickens and Poe do, the former by means of a general descriptive detail, the latter by a subjective impression.

Each student should write three leads. Small groups then discuss and edit the leads (if you have not divided the class into groups before, do so now), helping each student to choose the best one to fit the intended mood, diction, and tone of the composition.

Finally, students write the paper. It should be one page in length.

When the papers come in, have students exchange them within the small groups. Each reader should determine and write on the paper what mood the writer was apparently intending to convey. The readers should also circle striking original details that detract from the dominant mood.

After the students have seen their own papers, have students hand the papers in. Read several aloud to the class and have students try to determine what the speaker's tone is.

## *Marking Guidelines*

❖ *Diction.* Is the word choice sharp and clear? Is the kind of diction employed consistent throughout the paper?

❖ *Originality.* Is the character fresh and original? Is the presentation of the situation or event unique? Has the writer used a clever juxtaposition of ideas, words, or images? Do you feel that this is something you have not seen before?

✦ **Unity.**  Does a strong, clear lead establish a dominant mood? Does the mood continue throughout the paper? (It is possible to change the mood, but that change must be clear and smooth.) Has the writer included any details that jar, or that undercut the mood?

**Sample Essay**

### NIK

*Walking through this park irritates me to the point where I want to hit the other people walking by. They think the fall colors are so lovely, they are not; it's just a bunch of dead leaves, dropping off an old decaying tree. So what? People love to tromp through this park when the air is cold and wind is hissing through the hanging branches. Children scamper across my path, flying kites and tripping me; dogs chomp at my feet while their owners run off to a game of Frisbee; and ice cream vendors try and push their frozen chemical compounds on defenseless humans. I have been in this park longer than any of them, but they all act as if this park was built solely for their enjoyment. All of them leaving paper, droppings, and junk to cover this lot, which I will have to spend long tiring hours cleaning up. They have no respect for a gentleman such as I.*

—LAURA LINDNER

**Comments.**  We learn much about character and mood in this short piece about a park cleaner. The word choice is generally vigorous, including some strong verbs. There is some inconsistency of diction, though: "a bunch of dead leaves" contrasts with "frozen chemical compounds." But the writer intends to show Nik as pretentious (see last sentence); perhaps inconsistencies help. The conception is original and powerful. The writer has put herself in an interesting place and has described it vividly. From the unifying lead through the details of many kinds, she produces feelings of anger and injury that remain with a reader when the paragraph is over. Although the paragraph could use further development, it communicates economically and forcefully.

UNIT SIX
# SLANTING A PORTRAIT

### ELEMENTS OF GOOD WRITING
### Audience, Diction, Originality

In this unit, students learn about the power of careful diction. By choosing words that have a consistent connotative slant, student writers can influence or direct the point of view of their audience.

In the main writing assignment, students will select people that they actually know (not public figures or television personalities) and about whom they may have strong positive or negative feelings. Each writer must know the chosen person well enough to be able to supply a large number of details concerning the subject's personality. Eventually students will write two portraits of their subjects, one favorable and one unfavorable.

***Discussion.*** Before class members choose subjects, conduct an activity using the board or overhead projector. Let the class help you create a character. Perhaps someone will provide an imaginative description. Or, to involve more students, you may prefer to build the imaginary character bit by bit. Ask questions such as, "Female or male?" "Young or old?" "Tall or short?" "How intelligent?" "Outgoing?" "How does she (he) dress?" and accept the first answer you hear, or the cleverest answer, or the most complete. Write the details in a list on the board. Have the class invent a name for the character.

When the list is complete, explain to the class the meanings of denotation and connotation. *Denotation* is the dictionary definition of a word. *Connotation* is the aura of implied or associative meanings that surround a word after it has been used for some time. All words have denotations. Most have connotations, too. Even the chemical term hydrogen, for instance, has come to possess connotations—ominous ones since the development of the hydrogen bomb.

Some words have connotations that communicate the same meaning to most of the members of a society. For example, the term *critic*, denotatively a judge, has negative connotations for most Americans today. Other words have private connotations for us, connotations arising from our own experiences. A friend finds that the word *organic* has unpleasant connotations for her—probably because she once bit into worms in an apple advertised as "organically grown."

It is only the public, not the private, connotations that are useful in this exercise. Furthermore, although words can connote quite specific things (for example, evil, joy, sorrow, warmth), for this assignment, connotations should be classified simply as favorable or unfavorable.

Explain to the class that you and they are going to create two word-portraits of the subject from the list on the board. One will be favorable, the other unfavorable. Go down the list with the class and remove all of the terms that are already judgmental or heavily connotative. Replace them with neutral terms if you can (for example replace "generous" with "free with money"—a phrase that could be either favorable or unfavorable, depending on context; and replace "ugly" with "distinctively featured").

Next choose a detail that will permit both favorable and unfavorable connotative synonyms. If one detail is "wealthy," for instance, the class could find a range of connotative terms, from "prosperous" or "well-off" through "filthy rich." Rank the terms from one extreme (favorable) to the other (unfavorable). Repeat the process with several more terms from the list. Linger on terms or perspectives that are *original*.

**Preliminary Writing.** When the students get the idea, divide the class in half. Assign for homework a word-portrait of the imaginary character that the class has created. Half of the class will write a favorable portrait; the other half will write an unfavorable one.

**Discussion.** Compare results the next day, discussing the connotative differences in the *diction* used in both kinds of portraits. The class should quickly see the power that word choice possesses. To illustrate how this power can influence our minds, you could show the class a description of a public figure in a news magazine or a tabloid newspaper. By selection of details and choice of words, the writers try to color our view of the figure. Have the class spot words employed for their connotative value and then replace those words with more neutral synonyms or with their connotative opposites. How does the description change?

Understanding of *audience* may emerge from a look at contemporary advertising. Advertisers try to influence the minds of their audiences: they try to direct consumers to buy the product or service that they are selling. Of course, connotative language is a potent weapon for the advertiser.

Tell each student to bring in a full-page ad from a newspaper or magazine.

First of all, advertisers must identify their audience. Have several students hold up their ads, and ask the class what audience the ad is intended for. In some cases (for example, ads for beer, sugar cereals, motorcycles, vacation resorts), students should easily be able to identify and describe the advertiser's audience; in others (such as those for television sets or charity donations), students may have trouble since the audience aimed at is more general. Ask the class to pick from the ads some words that make connotative appeals to the audience.

Having identified the audience, an advertiser adopts a certain tone. The tone, which expresses the relationship between the ad and the audience, may be chummy and inviting ("C'mon down!"), challenging ("Are you man enough to tame this 500 cc. Ripsnorter?"), snobby ("so exquisite, only the most discerning can afford it"), and so on. Again, ask some students to show their ads and talk about the various tones that the ad writers have chosen. What reasons dictated the choice of tone? Does connotative diction help establish the tone?

After students have grasped the concept of audience in advertising, return to the word-portraits of the class-created imaginary character. Ask students to try to identify the audience as you read some of the papers aloud.

Because you did not ask students to write for a specific audience, most of the papers will be directed generally, and students will not be able to say much about the audience at all. But slangy diction in one may aim the paper at a youthful audience. Or one of the portraits may be formal in diction and sentence structure, suitable for an audience more educated than a general group.

Most papers will probably adopt a neutral tone, which is usually appropriate for a general audience. But some may be abrupt or condescending or familiar toward the audience. If so, dwell on those papers. Ask how the tone is achieved. Is it consistent? Is it appropriate for the audience?

**Prewriting.** Students now choose their subjects for the main writing activity. Each student must know the subject well and should have strong positive or negative feelings about that person. To avoid embarrassment and vindictiveness, the subjects should *not* come from the class or from the students' immediate families. Students should invent neutral-sounding names for their characters.

Each student should make a list of details about the subject down the middle of a page. The terms used should be as neutral in connotation as possible. When the list is complete, the student makes two more lists. To the left of each central detail should be a favorable connotative synonym (a word or phrase) and to the right, one with unfavorable connotations. Students should arrange the details logically (all physical descriptions together, for example) and according to some sort of order (least to most revealing, or physical to mental to emotional, or common to unique). Look for original ideas and details.

**Writing.** Both portraits should be about one page long. Real names of the subjects should not be used. You might wish to have students circle their connotative word choices.

When the papers are finished, have students read them aloud. Without identifying which is which, students should read both portraits consecutively. The class should easily be able to tell which portrait is favorable and which is unfavorable. In discussion, try to identify the audience in each case. Find some words that describe the writer's tone. Comment on connotative effects and single out particularly striking original details.

### *Marking Guidelines*

* *Diction.* Is there a sharp, significant, and consistent connotative difference between the words used in the two portraits? Are there enough connotative words to convey the writer's point of view? Are the words accurate?

* *Audience.* Can a reader identify the intended audience? Are the diction and sentence structure appropriate to that audience? Is there a clear relationship between the speaker and the audience, a tone that can be expressed in words? Is the tone consistent throughout?

* *Originality.* Are there some original (not cliché or common to most of the class) details in the portraits? Are the details arranged in a clever or interesting order?

### *Sample Word Portrait*

> *Bruno is an adolescent male whose distinguishing feature is his surly manner. Stout and squat, Bruno feels that to get what he*

wants he must throw his weight around. Once in a while some unsuspecting student will get in his way and suffer humiliating consequences. Beads of filthy sweat and saliva ooze down Bruno's chin until quite a lather foams up. Then the poor unfortunate will be brutally pummeled to the ground, taken aback in complete surprise. In other words, Bruno is a terribly malicious bully.

Once he stares at you through his thick-lensed glasses, those piglike eyes hold you at their mercy. Bruno's appearance is unkempt, or to put it bluntly, he is a total slob. Greasy uncombed hair grows in inconsistent lengths atop a fatty round head, shielding in part an oily face speckled with unsightly acne. Breathing heavily and munching on a chocolate bar, Bruno announces his approach well in advance, let alone his hideous stench. Horribly wrinkled and filthy, his clothes are in total disarray.

Despite his generally grimy condition, it is evident that Bruno has extremely high opinions of himself. Obnoxiously he exclaims that he will someday become an enormously profound man in history, looking far down upon his peers. Not knowing or actually caring what goes on in the hidden mind of Bruno, everyone laughs at what they feel to be his plight.

—MAX DRAKE

**Comments.** In this piece, both connotative and denotative words produce a negative impact. Some words stand out: "squat," "ooze," "piglike," "oily," "wrinkled." In addition to these and other adjectives, the adverbs make the subject seem unpleasant. But economy suggests that, if the verbs, nouns, and adjectives are doing their job, the writer need not depend on words like "horribly," "terribly," and "enormously." It is interesting to note that in this context of unfavorable terms, even a neutral word like "adolescent" has an unfavorable cast. The writer's audience is apparently general, although some words ("malicious," "hideous," "profound") may not be within reach of everyone. Sentence variety makes the piece original, as does the writer's sharp focus on specific images and even smells. Despite a few problems in phrasing ("let alone . . . ," "everyone . . . they"), the portrait communicates clearly.

UNIT SEVEN
# DESCRIBING A PROCESS

### ELEMENTS OF GOOD WRITING
### Active Voice, Audience, Coherence

Describing a process—that is, writing a step-by-step explanation of how to do something—is a task that most of us perform many times in life. We may want to give a friend a recipe for mince pie or tell a relative how to get from San Francisco to San Jose. If our instructions are to be useful, they must be systematic and absolutely clear. If they are fuzzy or if details are out of order, the result may be mince mush or a trip to Sacramento—and an angry friend or relative.

***Discussion.*** Introduce the concept of process. An interesting way to do this is to find a set of directions for an imported small appliance or a small device that comes in a kit. For example, here are directions for setting a cheap imported digital clock:

*To set clock, there are three buttons. First button is hours. Hold button down until right hour. Second button is minutes. Hold until minutes beyond actual time. Now hold down third button which stops clock. When actual minutes arrives, let go. Clock is set.*

The directions that you find, like those for the clock, may be vague and contain peculiarities of diction and idiom; maybe you can even find a set with steps out of order. In any case, hold the object up and slowly read the directions to the class. Let students identify the ambiguous, misleading, or incomplete parts of the directions as you read them several times (or duplicate them). Have the class try to improve the weak parts.

***Preliminary Writing.*** As homework, assign a short paper (one page) that describes a moderately complicated process. You choose the process, one that requires simple materials and can be carried out in the classroom or school. As the students write, they should assume that their audience is totally ignorant of the process.

Two classic assignments are "How to Make a Peanut Butter and Jelly Sandwich" and "How to Make a Paper Airplane." The former produces some unappetizing creations with jelly smeared on the edges of the bread or peanut butter carefully spread on a desk top.

To test the results of airplane directions, you can hold a contest to see if any of the planes fly and, if so, how far (the most bizarre designs often go farthest).

**Discussion.** Have students exchange papers and have several students carry out the instructions in front of the class. If there are ambiguities, encourage the student following the instructions to misunderstand rather than to do what experience says is right.

Analyze the reasons for the failure of some of the sets of directions. Have the class suggest improvements.

**Prewriting.** Before students go off to compose the main writing assignment, review with them the three elements that are especially important in process. First, although it is sometimes difficult and even awkward, students should cast their process descriptions in the *active voice*. A list of directions such as "First the potatoes are boiled for 10 minutes, then they are diced, and then the basil and minced garlic are added" is monotonous and unemphatic. The most direct way that students can achieve active structures is to use the second person, which includes imperatives and allows variety: "Boil the potatoes for 10 minutes. Then dice them before you sprinkle on basil and garlic." Some process topics lend themselves to active third-person development—"Giant rollers press the pulp into sheets"—and these topics usually produce the most vigorous writing.

The next important consideration is *audience*—for whom is the description intended? Having identified the audience, the writer must match diction to it: no technical jargon, unless the audience will understand it perfectly; all words chosen to suit the age and experience of the people who will follow the directions. The principle of clear and economical communication is vital to writing about process; there is not the slightest room for ambiguity or incoherence.

Finally, *coherence* in a process is generally the result of careful chronological organization. If the steps are listed in the proper order, coherence is strong. But transitions are important, even if the mere order of the steps determines the coherence. In the description of a process, transitions often carry key information. Not only do phrases such as "after the puck has crossed the blue line," "three traffic lights beyond the Mobil station," and "before you add the clams" lead us from one detail to another, but they are vital details themselves. Outlining to ensure accurate sequence of details and checking the precision of transitions are the writer's tools for coherence.

**Writing.** Each student is to describe a process that he or she enjoys participating in. (Examples: how to dance the . . ., how to ride a horse, how to get to the stadium, how to develop photographs, how to eat an ice cream sundae.) Explain that the point of the assignment is to describe the process or activity with such precision and coherence that the audience will readily comprehend the steps.

The first homework assignment is an outline. You could specify the type of outline (topic outline or sentence outline) or allow students to choose a form. Check the outlines only superficially, but ask students to be sure that they have listed steps in the proper order. Then tell them to write a draft of a thesis statement that will attract the audience right from the start. Have several statements read aloud.

Students write the paper at home, rewriting the thesis statement if necessary. The paper should be two pages in length.

## *Marking Guidelines*

❖ *Active voice.* Has the writer used the active voice most of the time?

❖ *Audience.* Can one discern a specific audience for which the composition is intended? Are diction, tone, and sentence structure appropriate to that audience? The writer may be addressing a general audience; if so, diction and sentence structure should be clear and economical and the tone neutral.

❖ *Coherence.* Are details in proper (usually chronological) order? Are any details out of place? Are transitions adequate in number, clear, and precise? Is person (first, second, or third) consistent throughout?

## *Sample Essay*

### MAKING A CAKE

Making a cake requires precise measurements and the combining of good ingredients: fresh eggs, soft butter or margarine, flour, sugar, salt, vanilla, and baking powder.

Your first step is weighing four eggs, accurately, remembering the measurement. Put the eggs aside. Pour out enough sugar to equal the weight of the eggs. Tip the sugar into a large mixing bowl. Butter or margarine goes next into the mixing bowl. Blend the butter and sugar until they are creamy and smooth.

Measure the eggs' weight of flour, adding a teaspoon of vanilla, a dash of salt, and two tablespoons of baking powder. Combine several scoops of this mixture with the batter, mixing it until all is blended.

You're now ready to crack in an egg. This is done by cupping the egg firmly in your hand and bringing it down firmly on the edge of a counter, creating a crack by which you pull the eggshell apart. Mix the batter once again, blending the egg in. Continue alternately adding flour mixture and egg in small proportions, blending after each addition, until all the ingredients are in the batter. The batter, by now, should be light and frothy. If it is not, beat the mixture for several minutes.

Turn on the oven to 350°. While you wait for the oven to heat, prepare to grease the pan. Obtain wax paper and some fat. Using the wax paper to spread the fat, cover the bottom and sides of the pan.

Grasping the mixing bowl firmly, pour the contents into the greased pan. With the aid of a spatula, scrape the bowl clean. Avoid dribbling batter on upper parts of the pan as the spills burn into the pan.

When the oven is preheated, place the pan with batter in the center. After thirty minutes baking time, check the cake to see if it is fully cooked. Poke a skewer into the center of the cake. If batter sticks to the skewer, allow another three minutes to bake, and check again. If no batter sticks, remove the cake from the oven and allow it to cool.

—RACHEL SIMONS

**Comments.** Although writers often have great difficulty avoiding the passive voice in such process accounts, this writer has done well to use only a few passive constructions. Here the active voice pulls the audience (a general audience—the writer has avoided cooking jargon) into the account, and makes the account itself more direct and economical. This process, like most, is organized chronologically; transitions are plentiful and clear.

Even though the topic is not intrinsically exciting, the writer's presentation of it is vigorous. This process, written from personal experience, compares favorably to many cookbook presentations.

A comment on the paper should include the suggestion that the writer relies too heavily on participial phrases. She should replace some of them with subordinate clauses.

UNIT EIGHT
# DEFINING WORDS AND IDEAS

### ELEMENTS OF GOOD WRITING
### Audience, Clarity, Development, Diction

This unit provides practice in definition, a basic component of clear, economical communication. All too often learning writers fail to define a term that is vital to a reader's accurate understanding of the written work. In many cases, a writer's notion of the meaning of a term varies from a standard dictionary definition, and a reader may not recognize the aberrant usage on a first or second reading. Then, too, a dictionary definition may not include enough detail and may not account for important connotative meanings. Clear definition requires complete definition—development sufficient to achieve full communication.

The focal points of this unit are two papers. The first, one page long, defines something concrete; the second, a longer composition, defines an abstraction.

**Discussion.**  The act of definition is the act of drawing lines or boundaries around a word, an object, or an idea. These lines accomplish two things: they clearly enclose the term defined and they eliminate anything else.

The first step in drawing the lines of definition is to establish the *class* of things to which the term belongs. For example, a whale is an aquatic mammal; a pen is a writing implement; joy is an emotional state. Everything outside of the named class is excluded, cut out by the lines.

Next, other lines, called *qualifiers*, are drawn. Qualifiers tighten the definition—the more qualifiers accurately used, the less change of ambiguity. There are many kinds of qualifiers. Some common examples are *size, shape, color, composition, function, origin,* and *similarity*. Sometimes these qualifying lines may be combined (for example: "flared like an axe head" combines shape and similarity).

**Prewriting.**  Pick an object and have the class work out a list of lines of definition for it. For example:

DEFINING WORDS AND IDEAS 91

| OBJECT | LINES OF DEFINITION | |
|---|---|---|
| Glockenspiel | *Class* | Musical instrument |
| | *Subclass* | Percussion, marching |
| | *Size* | Portable, 4 × 3 feet |
| | *Shape* and *similarity* | Like lyre, but steel bars |
| | *Origin* | Old celesta |
| | *Range* | 2½ octaves |
| | *Tone* | Bright, penetrating |
| | *Differences* | Xylophone (wood bars not steel) Chimes (tubes not bars) |

Then choose a different object and demonstrate how some of the lines that were necessary to define the first object are inappropriate for defining the second; therefore the definer must find new lines.

For homework, have students choose three items from a list of objects. They should find lines of definition that explain each object clearly. You may wish to specify that they find six or eight different lines (including class) for each object.

To build clarity and precision, it is important to know the audience for this prewriting exercise and for the paper that follows it. Explain that the audience is to be someone who is utterly ignorant about the specific objects to be defined, but someone who knows English well. You might suggest that writers prepare their papers for an audience of classmates who will willfully misunderstand them if they are vague or imprecise. Or you may wish to create for an audience a visitor from space who has learned English—or perhaps a programmed computer with a perfectly literal mind.

Students should hand in three lists, each with a column for lines of definition and a column for the details that define the particular object.

**Discussion.** Put some of the students' lists on the board. Ask the class if the development is adequate: Can the willful misunderstander really tell what the object is? Can the object be confused with anything else in its class? How about the word choice? Are the defining lines clear and accurate? Do the defining lines fit the object?

Discuss the dangers of ambiguity and the need to develop various lines of definition.

Finally, compare some of the student lists to what the dictionary says about the word. Point out the inadequacy of the bare dictionary definition and praise richness of development and originality in the students' lists.

**Writing.** Following are three assignments for one-page compositions. Depending on the demands of time and the class's mastery of definition, you might wish to use one, two, or all three of them.

1. Assign a one-page written definition of one of the objects for which the students made lists of definition lines. They should choose the object that they feel will allow for the fullest development. Emphasize that they are to write a coherent composition made up of one or more well-built paragraphs, not a list of sentences. Stress the need for clarity and consistent diction in the descriptions.

2. Pick a single object for everyone in the class to define. Make it something common, so that students can examine it as they write. It should be neither too simple nor too intricate. A paper clip, for example, makes a good challenge.

3. Choose a nonsense word, such as *protopondle*, *glurb*, or *randalion*, for the class to define. The results will be varied and amusing, and may show understanding of the use of lines of definition, but they will be hard to check for ambiguity and accuracy.

When the papers come in, have students exchange them. Readers should underline ambiguities in the papers and indicate the source of the ambiguity (poor phrasing, inaccurate diction, ideas out of order). Return the papers to the writers for editing before you collect them.

### *Marking Guidelines*

◆ *Clarity.* Is the definition free of ambiguity?

◆ *Diction.* Is the kind of diction consistent (no mixing of slang, jargon, or formal words)? Are words, especially adjectives, sharp and precise?

◆ *Development.* Has the writer employed enough lines of definition to show not only what the object is, but how it differs from others in its class?

◆ *Audience.* Could the reader unfamiliar with the object learn what it was? Has the writer presumed no knowledge of the object on the reader's part?

## Sample Definition

A paper clip is an object used to join sheets of paper. It consists of a smooth length of aluminum wire that is twisted upon itself three times in an oblong spiral, forming three rounded protruding sections. The spiral lies flat and abstractly resembles a trombone. A paper clip weighs approximately one gram and is about one inch long, with nearly a quarter of an inch of space between the two rounded protuberances that point in the same direction. The wire, unbent, would be about three inches long. A paper clip does not work by clamping the sheets of paper together as other types of clips do, but rather wedges paper between the two rounded parts that face in the same direction.

—PETER WHITE

**Comments.** The second sentence presents a clear description of a difficult three-dimensional concept. The key term, "oblong spiral," requires some work to comprehend, but it is accurate. Later in the paper, the writer deals less clearly with the clip's shape. The diction is consistent, although "protuberance" is difficult for a general audience. One might hope for sharper word choice in some cases ("object," "length"); however, the verbs are accurate and clear. Even though the paper is short, the writer has used a good number of lines of definition: use, composition, shape, comparison (the trombone image is very helpful), weight, difference, and process.

**Discussion.** Defining an abstraction—something you can't see or touch, like *terror* or *autumn*—is harder than defining something concrete. On the other hand, the writer's need for abstract definitions is usually greater than for concrete ones. Because abstractions may be surrounded by ambiguity and connotation, a writer must define them clearly.

In general, a writer defines an abstraction by the same process used to define an object. First, the writer finds the *class* to which the abstract term belongs (*terror* is an emotion; *autumn* is a season of the year). Then the writer adds the *qualifiers* that draw lines around it, separating it from other terms in its class.

The search for useful qualifying lines of definition may be difficult. The common lines, such as *size, composition,* and *function,* don't work very well with abstractions. Instead, the writer must find other lines. Perhaps an *anecdote* will help to define the abstraction *embarrassment*. A number of different *examples* defined the term *happiness* ("Happiness is . . . ") in a commercial definition of a decade ago. Some of the many other lines that might be useful in making abstractions clear are: *manifestation* (sweaty palms—nervousness), *analogy* (the halfback feeling like a lion—courage), and *association* (the melody of a wind in springtime—romance). Note that these lines of definition tend to supply concrete impressions to give the abstract terms tangibility.

**Prewriting.** *Student responsibility* is an abstraction that produces discussion at almost any school. Here it is used as a means of demonstrating the need for definition of abstractions. Ask students if they think that students should have more responsibility in running the school. If the response is positive, ask what several of them mean by *responsibility*. After a brief brainstorming session, each student is to write a one-paragraph definition of student responsibility.

Read some of the definitions aloud. Then compare them to what the dictionary says. Here is an abridgment of Webster's definition of *responsibility*, followed by a tenth-grader's paragraph, written in class:

> *Moral, legal, or mental accountability; . . . reliability, trustworthiness . . .*
> —WEBSTER'S *NEW COLLEGIATE*

> *Student responsibility is the act of every student having some say in what goes on in the community. Whether there's a problem in a student's class, or there is a mutual obstruction in the community, each student should feel he has enough confidence to stand up and say something about it. Student responsibility also says that each student must feel tied to any school-wide event, good or bad. Each student should feel that he has something to do with what goes on, and that he can help better or simply contribute to any situation. Giving responsibility to every student is a great honor, for it shows that the school has confidence in its students. Student responsibility also brings the school closer together.*
> —ANN COLEMAN

The student writer did not use terms like "accountability," "reliability," and "trustworthiness." Likely, neither did most of your students. There is a significant discrepancy between the students' sense of the key term responsibility and the meaning that reflects the usage of society at large.

**Discussion.** Out of this discovery should grow both a lesson on the necessity to use the dictionary and an understanding of how important it is to define essential terms. It is generally not enough to define one abstraction with others, as the dictionary does. One must go farther to assure communication with the audience.

Have students exchange paragraphs. Then ask them to identify the lines of definition in the paragraph before them. How many lines are there? Are those lines appropriate to the audience? A common line of definition is *example*—student responsibility in a given situation. In the student sample above, there are a number of lines of example, although the examples are themselves general ones. Ask students to list aloud the lines they have found. (Other lines in the sample are *method, feeling,* and *effect.*) The writer who follows several lines of definition, and makes clear transitions between them, is far more likely to communicate effectively to an audience than the writer who depends solely on other abstractions to define the term.

**Writing.** Each student is to define an abstract term, without naming that term in the paper. The audience is presumed to be ignorant of the term. The reader might be a beginning driver who has never felt *horror* at seeing the carnage of a bad automobile accident or a Southern Californian who has never experienced the exhilaration of the first snowfall in New England.

Although the paper need not be formal in tone, students should follow the methods of definition. Remind them to find useful lines of definition. Insist on qualifiers that draw exclusive boundaries. Encourage students to approach their selection of lines and details with originality.

Students should choose their own abstractions and then check them with you. Be sure that the terms are indeed abstract and that they hold promise of interesting development.

The paper should be one-and-a-half pages long. Adequate development depends on the inclusion of sufficient details to explain the various lines of definition. Clarity requires that those details communicate economically and vividly: precise diction is essential. Some of the details may be subjective. The test of subjective details is how well, if at all, they bring the private world of the writer's own experience to a reader. If the reader is baffled, the details probably lack clarity, and the definition suffers.

When the papers come in, have them read aloud and see if students can accurately name the abstractions in each other's papers.

### Marking Guidelines

* *Audience.* Do the writer's definition lines indicate that the paper is designed for a general audience?
* *Clarity.* Are the details easily comprehensible? Is the definition unambiguous?
* *Development.* Has the writer used enough lines of definition to show what the abstraction is and to eliminate other related abstractions?
* *Diction.* Is word choice clear, sharp, and accurate?

### Sample Definition

> In the heavenly realm, it is the area or region beyond the earth's atmosphere, beyond the solar system; visible but unlimited, thought about but unknown, everywhere but unexplored. It exists, still, motionless, omnipresent, while various stars, planets, and heavenly bodies move continuously through its perpetual darkness.
>
> Within the earthly realm, it is a limited area, distance, volume—set apart, available, or unoccupied. It has many divers meanings, such as an area between two parked cars that enables you to park your car. It can be the amount of room on a floor or in a closet. It is also the area taken up by an individual where in many cases the individual becomes angry or perturbed when others encroach upon or crowd it.
>
> It can also be applied domestically, as in the use of a typewriter or telegraph transmission. It is designated a special key on the typewriter, extending lengthwise across the bottom of the keyboard. It is used to separate the last letter of one word from the first letter of the next word. Likewise, in a telegraph transmission it is the interval in operation during which the key is not in contact with the rest of the mechanism. It is incorporated in both the typewriter and the telegraph for the purpose of distinguishing one word from the next.
>
> —JIM GILE

**Comments.** In diction and choice of example, this definition of the abstract noun *space* is appropriate for a general audience. Examples that extend from the heavens to the earth approach the abstraction along a number of lines: location, shape, function, effect, and purpose. Development proceeds from the very broad (first paragraph, topic sentence of second paragraph) to the specific—an effective method of organization. Note that the multiple lines allow for clear communication even though one of the details (end of paragraph two) is presented in a muddled manner.

# UNIT NINE
# COMPARING OBJECTS AND CONCEPTS

### ELEMENTS OF GOOD WRITING
### Coherence, Development, Originality, Unity

Many academic assignments call for skill in drawing comparisons. Compositions written about historical events and about literature often contain literal comparisons, while a writer who needs to explain difficult concepts or scientific principles may use figurative comparisons, or analogies, to communicate. Although direct comparisons are useful far more often than analogies, an original analogy makes a memorable impact on an audience. In this unit, students write papers using both literal comparisons and figurative analogies.

***Discussion.*** For preliminary writing, ask students to compare, in a paragraph, two objects, such as:
  ◊ a volleyball and a soccer ball
  ◊ a paper clip and a staple
  ◊ a skateboard and a pair of roller skates
  ◊ an apple and an orange

Students who are learning to write need help in maintaining clarity and balance when they make comparisons. Such help is available in the form of two model structures, called *block* and *shuttle*, for comparison and contrast. Each of these structures has its uses and problems; some of these are apparent when you put the two forms on the board. Oranges and apples are compared in this skeleton model, which shows only the key terms and the transitions.

### BLOCK COMPARISON

Apples . . . . . . . . . . . . . . . . . than oranges. Apples . . . . . . . . . . . . .
. . . . .; they . . . . . . . . . . . . . . . . . . apples . . . . . . . . . . . . . . . . .
Apples . . . . . . . . . . . . . . . . They . . . . . . . . . . . . . . . . . apples
. . . . . . . . . . . . . . . . . . apples.
  On the other hand, oranges . . . . . . . . . . . . . . . . . . than apples.
Oranges . . . . . . . . . . . . . . . . . . They . . . . . . . . . . . . . . . . . . .
oranges . . . . . . . . . . . . . . . . . Oranges . . . . . . . . . . . . . . . . . .;
they . . . . . . . . . . . . . . . . . oranges.

### SHUTTLE COMPARISON

Apples . . . . . . . . . . . . . . . . . . than oranges. They . . . . . . . . . . . . .
. . . . ., whereas oranges . . . . . . . . . . . . . . . . . . Apples . . . . . . . .
. . . . . . . . . rather than . . . . . . . . . . . . . . . . . . as oranges . . . . . .
. . . . . . . . . . . apples. Just as oranges . . . . . . . . . . . . . . . . . ., so
apples . . . . . . . . . . . . . . . . . . But oranges . . . . . . . . . . . . . . . . .,
while apples . . . . . . . . . . . . . . . . . Oranges . . . . . . . . . . . . . . . .
. . although . . . . . . . . . . . . . . . . . . apples . . . . . . . . . . . . . . . . . .
Apples . . . . . . . . . . . . . . . . . . than oranges, but oranges . . . . . . . .
. . . . . . . . . than apples.

As a glance at the forms indicates, the block method is simpler for a writer to use than the shuttle method. After a topic or thesis statement that makes a general comparison, the writer makes all points about apples in the first section and then writes a transitional sentence and tries to balance the points about apples with points about oranges in the second section.

The shuttle method, on the other hand, requires going back and forth about apples and oranges, often in the same sentence. Shuttling between the two objects requires absolutely accurate syntax, and, if it is not to bore the reader, it demands variety in the use of transitional devices. While the shuttle method risks confusion, it does assure a balanced comparison since every basis of comparison is applied to both objects, one right after the other.

Actually, most comparisons use a combination of block and shuttle. But for the sake of control and discipline, learning writers should use them separately at first.

***Preliminary Writing.*** Put on the board the list of topics such as those on page 97. Tell students to choose either the block or shuttle structure for their paragraphs. Remind them that coherence in the assignment depends on the effective use of transitions. Transitions occur within each sentence of the shuttle form, whereas in the block form a single strong transition in the middle takes the reader from one object to another.

***Discussion.*** Have students exchange their paragraphs. Ask the readers first to determine if the form used is block or shuttle. This determination should be easy; if it is not, the writer has probably mixed block and shuttle, at the risk of confusing the reader.

Then ask readers to underline transitional words and phrases. Ask a number of students to read aloud the transitions in the papers they are working on, and write the transitions on the board to reinforce the students' understanding of what transitions are and how they work in a paragraph.

**Prewriting.** As a prewriting exercise, have the class choose two comparable things (two television shows, two towns, two team sports). On the board list the attributes of each in parallel columns. From the lists try to draw a general basis for comparison between the two objects and state that basis in a sentence (for example, "Although Penrose High is a small school in a quiet town, its students are more active than those in its larger neighbor, Fillmore High."). Then check off the attributes that help to support the comparison and contrast. When an item in one column is not balanced by one in the other, add the balancing item to the second column (if the size of Penrose is given, but not that of Fillmore, add the size of Fillmore).

Unity demands such balance between the two sides of the comparison. Remind students that unity also means that no irrelevant details are present in the comparison. As in all writing, a strong thesis statement is a great help.

Now have the class write a comparison of the two things on the board. All students work together to compose a thesis statement that you write on the board. Then half of the class develops the comparison by the block method and half by the shuttle. Students should use all of the listed details.

**Discussion.** Compare the results, focusing on the merits and difficulties of each method. Also look for coherence: appropriate ordering of details and transitions between those details. Find an example of a well-unified paper in which the writer has included no irrelevant or unbalanced details.

**Writing.** For the final paper, which should be two pages long, you might wish to assign for comparison and contrast two subjects that will require some research (two musical instruments, two novelists, two African tribes). Or you might prefer to assign a more familiar topic so that they can concentrate on organization and writing.

Emphasize the need for thorough development. The length of the paper implies that superficial treatment of the two things compared is not enough. Students must support their generalizations with details, enough details so that the audience can really come to comprehend the two things and thereby perceive their similarities and differences.

As the length of the comparison increases, the demand for strict balance changes. Although the writer should continue to seek equivalent details on both sides of the comparison, the important balance is one of space. Writers should seek out what is most significant about the two things and then devote roughly equal space to each thing. Such a procedure means that the comparison might not be point by point throughout the paper. It also means that the shuttle structure will probably be inappropriate. (In any case, it is difficult to sustain a shuttle comparison for very long.) A mix of block and shuttle is possible; however, the writer should beware of shifting from block to shuttle and back more than once.

Here are some sample topics for the papers. You might wish to augment the list or to use topics of your own. In any case, students must examine the topics they choose to determine appropriate scope. With or without your help, they must make their topics narrow enough so that adequate development that goes beyond superficiality is possible.

- My Public Self and My Private Self
- Reading the Book and Seeing the Movie
- Commuting by Car and Commuting by Bike
- Music on the Radio and Music at the Concert Hall
- AM and FM Radio
- The World as I See It and the World as My Parents See It
- Long Distance Phone Calls and Letters
- Television News and Newspaper News
- Fast Food and Home-Cooked Food
- Dostoevski's *Notes from the Underground* and Ellison's *Invisible Man*
- Team Sports and Individual Sports
- Buying Something and Making Something Myself
- Osage and Hopi Religious Rites
- Soviet and U.S. Marriage Customs
- Robinson Jeffers's "Haunted Country" and Robert Frost's "Directive"
- A Monet and a Renoir Landscape
- The Piano and the Harpsichord
- Opera and Movie Musicals
- Canadian and U.S. Football
- Dress in America in 1975 and Now

## Marking Guidelines

♦ *Coherence.* Are details arranged in some sort of logical order? Are transitions clear, accurate, and sufficient in number? Is there variety in the transitions?

♦ *Development.* Is the topic narrow enough to permit full development? Has the writer used enough details to support all generalizations?

♦ *Unity.* Do all of the details pertain to the thesis statement? Is there a balance between the two things compared?

## Sample Comparison

### GRANOLA INFORMATION

*Being a frequent granola eater, I am capable of distinguishing between good and bad kinds of granola. Two drastically different brands that immediately come into mind are Quaker 100% Natural Cereal and the granola served at Draper Hall.*

*The chunks of varied sizes that comprise Quaker 100% Natural Cereal create a pleasant diversity in texture, whereas Draper granola's tiny bits have the consistency of sand. Milk added to a bowl of Quaker 100% Natural does not take on a rusty brown color, as does milk contaminated by Draper's granola. Unlike the rich flavor of Quaker 100% Natural, the flavor of Draper's granola is neutralized by excessive amounts of sugar. The freshness of Quaker 100% Natural enables it to function as a crisp salad topping, a refreshing trail mix, or a crunchy cereal. On the other hand, Draper's granola is far too soggy and stale to give life to anything. Where Quaker 100% Natural is chock-full of big, moist raisins, Draper's scanty raisins are extremely shriveled and so brittle that they crack when one bravely attempts to chew them. Adding a different flavor and another texture to Quaker 100% Natural, the abundant dates are soft and chewy. The dehydrated dates contained in Draper's granola, however, gradually flake apart when placed in one's mouth.*

*Most granola fans adore the natural taste and original texture of Quaker 100% Natural Cereal, so when purchasing granola for an enemy, Draper's granola is the better choice.*

—WENDY SHAPIRO

**Comments.** This pleasant informal essay is rather short for the assignment, but it nicely demonstrates the use of extended shuttle development. When a writer uses the shuttle form, the reader must make quick correspondences from one item to another; it is hard to keep a sense of the organizational scheme in mind. Hence coherence in the shuttle pattern depends less on logical sequence of ideas—although the ideas must not jar—than on effective transitional phrases. Here there is no apparent order of details (one might expect "uses" to conclude the middle paragraph, but it does not occur that way); however the transitions are clear and nicely varied. Development is suited to the topic: we probably want to know this much about the two kinds of granola, but no more. The details are precise and lively, pertinent to the comparison. The shuttle form assures a balance in the comparison. The writer supplies an original, delightful reversal at the end.

**Discussion.** An analogy works much as a literal comparison does, although it is used as an illustration rather than as a means of proof or argument. But while both objects are discussed equally in a literal comparison, the writer of an analogy counts on the reader's familiarity with one object in the comparison to help explain points about the unfamiliar object. That is, the essential difference is that in a literal comparison the two objects are similar, of the same sort or type or class, while in an analogy they are essentially dissimilar and the comparison is figurative or metaphorical.

In a metaphor, two dissimilar objects possess a common characteristic. In the midst of his despair with life, Shakespeare's Macbeth says, "Out, out, brief candle." The life of man and a candle's flame are utterly dissimilar; yet one shared characteristic—how easily each may be extinguished—tells us memorably how Shakespeare's character detests his prospects. The metaphor conveys a complex emotion in a few clear words.

In an analogy, the two objects are essentially dissimilar, as they are in a metaphor; but they share several characteristics, not just one. A common analogy used in science classes is the explanation of the propagation of radio waves by comparing it to the ripples in a pond caused by a pebble thrown into the water. Here correspondences are complex: the pebble is like the radio transmitter; the ripples in the pond are comparable to radio waves; the water and the air are both media through which the waves travel. The ripples radiate outward equally in all directions, have a certain wavelength, and weaken as they go—and so do radio waves. The science teacher adds details and elucidation so that the process will be clear to students. They come rapidly to understand how radio waves work because they have seen the ripples in the pond—the familiar used to explain the unfamiliar.

**Prewriting.** You can find material for a prewriting drill in the sports pages of the local newspaper or in a popular tabloid. Look for feature articles and stories written about games local teams have just played. Often a sportswriter, who is always searching for a fresh way to gain the audience's attention, will employ an analogy to describe the team's performance. The writer may compare the team to a sluggish bear, rising after hibernation, or to a puppy that trips over its feet. Some analogies will be clever and sustained through several paragraphs, while others will be clichés that last only a line or two. Read several to the class and have students find and bring in some analogies themselves. Have the class rank the analogies according to originality and effectiveness.

Then have students invent analogies, following the pattern of the sports pages, to describe the activities of groups they know. They may choose a school athletic team, the city government, or a musical group, for instance. They should develop the analogy in two to three paragraphs, being sure to use the familiar half of the comparison to characterize the unfamiliar (here, the activity of the group). As students read their analogies aloud, be sure the comparison is figurative and that the familiar and the unfamiliar are of different classes. One musical group should not be compared to another, for example—that would be a literal comparison.

**Writing.** The final writing assignment, which should be about one page long, requires that students compare themselves, or something about themselves, to nonbreathing objects. They might compare enthusiasm for English class to a three-way light bulb, or an attitude toward life to a sailboat in changing conditions of wind and water, or extracurricular interests to a subway system.

Success in communication by analogy depends not only on the appropriateness of the familiar object but also on the *originality* of the comparison. Writers should avoid the obvious, such as comparisons to rocks, trees, books, and so forth. A strikingly original comparison helps the writer to achieve clear, economical, and memorable communication.

As the students write, they should keep in mind that they are using the known object (the light bulb, the sailboat, the subway) to explain the unknown (themselves). They should also be aware that parts of the analogy other than the primary comparison should be developed, too—not just the sailboat, for instance, but the wind and water as well.

While parts of this unit are fun to do together with the class, be sure to treat the final analogies gingerly. Some will be privileged communications, and their writers will not want them shared with the whole class.

### Marking Guidelines

* *Development.* Is the analogy detailed? Has the writer developed ideas other than the central basis for comparison?
* *Originality.* Is the choice of object for comparison original? Has the writer developed it with ingenuity? Are any details especially memorable?

### Sample Comparison

> My temper is a tall oak tree. In its early stages it was easily snapped or bent, but as it grew, it became stronger and more stable. Now tall and sturdy, it holds fast and unbudging even in the worst of conditions. The tree is affected only when one constantly hacks away at one of the tree's limbs. If he is not careful, the limb may suddenly crash down on top of him. Or if the assailant decides to chop away at the base of the tree, the deeper he chops the more likely the tree will begin to lose its balance. If he goes too far, the tree will suddenly topple upon him and he may be severely hurt.
>
> As of now that has yet to happen. But as time goes on, the tree will grow and, in time, will become almost immovable.
>
> —LOUIS OZE

**Comments.** The writer has limited his subject, and within that scope has developed it adequately. His analogy makes not only the basic comparison of temper and oak tree but also a comparison between the process of losing his temper (even to the point of irrationality) and the process of chopping down the tree. Although the use of a tree is not highly original, the treatment of it is both novel and highly appropriate. The analogy forces the reader to look at the tree—and thence the temper—as an object subject to attack from without. The concept of potential power unleashed for damage (the falling tree, the out-of-control temper) is striking.

UNIT TEN
# ANALYZING A TELEVISION SHOW AND A BOOK

### ELEMENTS OF GOOD WRITING
### Active Voice, Audience, Sources, Unity

Ordered analysis is the goal of this unit, which includes two writing assignments: an analysis of a television program and a book review. Students must follow a clear and logical process from selection of subject matter through finished paper. In this process, they receive specific guidance from you; they should learn to apply similar analytical procedures to other writing tasks.

*Discussion.* Analysis implies a separation into parts. All things have parts, of course; the division must be logical and consistent. What are the parts of a grapefruit, for instance? Probably we would analyze a grapefruit into rind, pulp, meat, and seeds. We wouldn't examine its molecular structure or say simply that it possessed an outside and an inside.

Not all parts of a thing are physical. One might analyze an oil painting into the parts of frame, canvas, and paint. Such an analysis, however, is not helpful in understanding the painting. A student of art would be better served by dividing the painting into sections (foreground, middle ground, background), or into color patterns, or into light and shade, or into emphatic and supporting details.

The point of analysis is to clarify the relationships that exist among the parts of something and thereby to elucidate the meaning of the whole.

*Preliminary Writing.* Display a painting to the class. Almost any work will do, although representational paintings with plentiful details are more suitable for this activity than are abstract paintings with few details. The painting should be large—or perhaps you can project a slide of a painting so the whole class can see it clearly at one time.

Ask students to write a one-paragraph analysis of the painting. Do not tell them how to analyze it; let each student discover an approach.

***Discussion.*** After 20 minutes, collect the paragraphs. Read several aloud, asking the class each time to determine how the writer has analyzed the painting. Into what parts is the painting divided? Are the parts parallel and consistent? Is there a single organizing principle (such as the painting's purpose, or its dominant impression, or its color or shade patterns) that shapes the analysis?

Explain that the unity of an analysis depends heavily on the clear statement of a central idea, an idea that directs the development of the paragraph. Here are three topic sentences that suggest how the writer will develop a paragraph about a painting:

> *A radiant light illuminates two boys at rest in the middle of a field.*
>
> *In Renoir's painting the figures in the foreground are more important than the land and sea that surround them on three sides.*
>
> *Still water reflects the sprawling castle, its colors dulled slightly in the water.*

In each case we not only see the dominant impression that each of the three different paintings has made but also infer the parts into which the writer will divide the painting (light and space in the first case; figures, land, and sea in the second; castle and reflection in the third).

On the board, write some good topic sentences from the paragraphs the class has written. Seek especially those containing strong verbs in the active voice. Students should see how the active construction that employs a strong verb (like "illuminates" or "reflects" in the examples above) helps the writer make a clear, economical assertion about the picture.

***Preliminary Writing.*** Ask students to write another paragraph of analysis about a painting. You can use the same painting as before or a different one. This time, emphasize the need for a strong unifying topic sentence. Allow students to take notes on the picture in class if you assign the paragraph for homework.

***Discussion.*** When the paragraphs come in, put several topic sentences on the board for evaluation. Have the class look for strong verbs in active constructions.

Now the class will move from analysis of a painting, something fixed in space and time, to a more difficult assignment: analysis of a television show, which will not simply sit there while they think about it.

The procedure for introducing the topic is as follows. Briefly discuss some of the television programs that the students like to watch, trying to elicit as many titles as come easily from them. Then explain that this assignment requires that they each choose one half-hour show, of any kind whatsoever, which they believe others in the class may not be likely to see. The reason for this requirement is that they will not be able to assume that their audience is familiar with the subject matter and therefore they will have to define and describe it clearly.

***Prewriting.*** The class should take careful notes while you give them a scheme for the analysis of the show they will choose. The analysis has four parts: definition, recognition of aims, description, and assessment.

DEFINITION. Students must tell what class of program—news, sports, comedy, and so on—theirs belongs to. Then what sort of show it is within that class—situation comedy set in Harlem, outdoor show with this particular segment devoted to fly casting for trout, and so forth.

RECOGNITION OF AIMS. Students should explain what they believe the aims, intentions, or goals of the program are, and, in a general sense, how it goes about achieving these aims. Does the show try to amuse the audience through exaggeration and slapstick? Or inform by means of a number of different examples (scenes)? Or promulgate a certain message (what?) using sex appeal?

DESCRIPTION. Next comes an exposition of the specific methods the program employs to achieve its goals—what exactly goes on? For a drama, the description should include a brief plot outline but should focus on the specific means (scenes, characters, special effects) used in the show. If the show is full of violence, for example, specific scenes or events of violence should be discussed. If slapstick, the discussion should focus on specific acts that are intended to get laughs. If a news program, the discussion should include the ways in which specific stories are presented.

Here is an important opportunity to use sources to recreate for the audience the flavor of the show. As they watch the show, students should take notes that include actual quotations, such as short, typical exchanges of dialogue between characters. In their papers they should be sure to punctuate the quotations accurately and to introduce them with transitions.

Although description will be the paper's longest section, it should not be overwhelmingly so. A good guide for students to use is that the description should not be longer than any two other sections put together.

ASSESSMENT. Judgment is the last part of the analysis. It depends on what has gone before, on how thoroughly and effectively the program achieved the aims and intentions set forth in the second part of the analysis. In most cases, the assessment will be both objective and subjective. While it will rest on specific evidence from the program, it will be colored by the writer's individual perception, and that perception will be affected by past experience and prejudices. For instance, if the program is meant to amuse through burlesque, and the writer is not amused (for whatever reason—age, background, indigestion), the judgment will be at least partly negative. The writer should, however, strive to be as objective as possible.

Objectivity is the writer's duty to the audience. Effective communication depends on the maintenance of trust between writer and reader. If the reader feels that the writer is serving personal interests by impressing prejudices upon the analysis, that reader may well reject the entire review.

**Writing.** Students are to use the four-part structure presented above to write an analysis of a television show of their individual choosing. The analysis should be one-and-a-half to two pages long.

Emphasize that the papers must *build* to the judgment or assessment—no judgmental or prejudicial terms ("at the opening of this ridiculous program," "the most important element of this clever plot") should appear until the final part of the paper. Furthermore, in order that the final assessment be convincing, the writer must supply adequate details along the way. The reader should be able to make a judgment, too, based on material in the first three parts of the analysis.

### *Marking Guidelines*

❖ *Active voice.* Has the writer sought strong, active constructions? Does the writing avoid passive and expletive constructions?

❖ *Audience.* Is the language objective rather than prejudicial? Has the writer withheld judgment until the end of the analysis?

- *Sources.* Has the writer used one or more quotations to give the reader the flavor of the program? Are quotations introduced with transitions? Are they punctuated accurately?
- *Unity.* Is each topic sentence strong and clear? In the description section, does a topic sentence organize it clearly?

## Sample Analysis

> Say, Brother is a talk-show focused on the teen-age black community through a panel of high school students who are mostly black. The program offers assistance, consolation, and advice to viewers about problems that may present themselves, and often do, to teen-age blacks. Say, Brother researches these problems, acquires public opinion on them, and provides a forum by which members of the community (the panel) can help themselves.
>
> Say, Brother begins with face-to-face interviews with the public on an issue. Frank questions, pertinent to adolescent blacks, are posed, such as, "Where do you think sex should be taught: at home, in school, or in the streets?" The scene is then transferred to a moderately barren room (in order to direct attention towards its occupants) containing the host and a panel. "Do you think young people are getting pushed into sexual activity?" is an example of a question that the panel discusses. After ten or fifteen minutes the host allows viewers to call the studio and ask the panel questions. Such questions as, "Do you think the whole functional part of sex should be taught in school?" are phoned in. Next, Say, Brother's special segment, Say You, is presented. In this segment occur performances of African music, art exhibitions, and so forth. The show concludes with a brief summary of the episode by the host, and a list of additional sources that viewers may seek for help.
>
> The intentions of Say, Brother are noble and are usually achieved; however, even a troubled viewer might not be able to bear its non-professionalism. Members of the panel are sometimes very stupid, and the quality of directing is always less than that of other television shows. On the other hand, the troubled viewer might feel he could relate to some of the members on the panel. If you are teen-age, black, and troubled, Say, Brother may prove to be a desirable and very beneficial show to watch.
>
> —STUART WESTBROOK

**Comments.** The writer has generally employed the active voice in the analysis, but note how passive constructions in the second and third sentences of the second paragraph blunt the impact of those sentences. Two more passive constructions occur toward the end of that paragraph of description. Throughout the definition and recognition of aims sections (paragraph one) and in the description section, the writer successfully withholds judgment, although the details he presents do help to justify his judgment of "non-professionalism" in the assessment. Quotations are vivid; the sources help us understand what the program sounded like. Paragraphs one and three are helped by strong topic sentences. The middle paragraph lacks a clear topic sentence—perhaps because the writer did not find unity in the program itself.

**Discussion.** Although students may have written book reviews before, they must be careful to differentiate between them and their elementary school counterparts—book reports. A book report is a *summary* of the book: author, title, plot or contents. It bears the same relationship to the book as a comic book version does.

The book review, on the other hand, does not try to reproduce the book. Instead, it *defines*, *describes*, and *judges* the book. It is a much more sophisticated exercise because it demands discrimination, careful objectivity, and logical organization. Rather than following the structure of the book itself (chronological, or beginning to end), it has its own structure, its own set of steps.

As they read the books they have chosen, students should keep in mind that they will be writing a review that follows the same four steps of analysis—definition, recognition of aims, description, and assessment—as their analysis of a television program.

**Prewriting.** As they read their books, students should take notes. These notes should include:
- details that are important in the book's development or that typify the book's approach to its subject matter
- accurate quotations that students can use when they write
- generalizations about the book that occur to them as they read (e.g., "the author portrays women in a strong light," "honesty in speech is more important than anything else," "advertising has become more sophisticated while it has grown more corrupt")

These can help with the creation of good thesis statements later on.

For all three kinds of notes, they should include page numbers. These numbers will help them find references quickly and will aid them when they want to develop a general idea.

**Writing.** The book for review may be one assigned in common to the class. Or students may choose their own, but the books must be ones that they haven't read before. If time is a problem, you might have students review a short story. Because source material will be there at hand, the paper should be longer than the television analysis: about three pages.

Students should follow the same four-part structure that they used in the previous writing assignment. Remind them to concentrate on writing strong topic sentences, using the active voice.

Use of sources is vital. Be sure that students know how to punctuate accurately, and emphasize the need to introduce quotations. A transition like "We see the speaker's naiveté when he asks, 'What had an old slave to do with humanity?'" helps the writer use sources without drawing the reader to a halt.

If you want to ask students to use footnotes for their quotations, be sure that they know the proper format. Also let them know that you require that they adhere strictly to that form.

Finally, caution students to withhold their own biases from the body of the review. They may introduce some subjectivity into the ending assessment, although if they do so, they should make clear that the point of view is their own ("Although romances generally leave me cold, . . ." ". . . even though I do not believe weaponry is a viable deterrent . . .").

## Marking Guidelines

* *Active voice.* Has the writer employed active constructions with vigorous verbs rather than passive or expletive constructions, particularly in topic sentences?
* *Audience.* Is the review clear of bias until the assessment? Has the writer been able to withhold judgment until all the evidence has been presented? Is the vocabulary appropriate for a general audience?
* *Sources.* Has the writer used quotations to support generalizations? Are the quotations well chosen and sufficient in number to give a sense of the experience of reading the book? Are they punctuated accurately? If you have required footnotes, are the footnotes accurate in form?
* *Unity.* Do the paragraphs include strong organizing sentences? Does the assessment rely on the description?

## Sample Review

Ralph Ellison's novel Invisible Man *depicts the story of a young Black who leaves the South and travels to New York City. Through this story the hero struggles to recognize and achieve his own humanity, against the false images of himself which others force upon him.*

*The arrangement of the plot brings out the false images of the hero that others want him to be. It begins at the end, as a prologue in which the hero looks back on the story he is about to tell, setting a tone for the book as he explains what he means by "invisibility":*

> "I am invisible, understand, simply because people refuse to see me.... It is as though I have been surrounded by mirrors of hard, distorting glass. When they approach me they see only my surroundings, themselves, or figments of their imagination—indeed, everything and anything but me." (p. 3)

*Thus Ellison explains his major theme: the bitterness of the hero at being ignored and having false images put in his place.*

*The hero tells his life's story, in which the people around him lay down paths for him to follow. By acting as others expect, the hero allows them to see him as they wish, not as he really is.*

*After being expelled unjustly from his southern college, the hero travels to New York and eventually finds work in a paint factory. After being caught in a boiler explosion, he is put in the factory hospital, where he undergoes cruel shock treatments designed to change his personality. The treatments succeed in removing only his fear. The hero, who finds himself to be an effective orator, accepts a job for a left-wing political organization. When he realizes that the organization's aims for him are little different from those of the people who earlier controlled him, ignoring his wants, the hero becomes disillusioned. He tells a leader of the organization:*

> "Look at me! Look at me! ... Everywhere I've turned somebody has wanted to sacrifice me for my good—only they were the ones who benefited." (p. 494)

*He finally rejects his entire former life as he burns the papers which stood for its parts: his high school diploma, a paper with his false organization name on it, and so on.*

*The novel's greatness lies in how well Ellison portrays the theme of invisibility throughout the novel. It is a universal theme; all of us must fight to assert ourselves against those who want to control us or fit us to their purposes. Although the plot of* Invisible Man *falters in spots (what paint factory has its own hospital?), its vivid symbolism and well-handled themes make it an awesome achievement.*

—ART SMALL

**Comments.** Vigorous, well-subordinated sentences make this a strong piece of writing. The writer has generally avoided passive and expletive constructions (there is one in paragraph four). Judgment of the novel occurs, as it should, only at the end of the review. However, the writer should have further developed the assessment (what "vivid symbolism"?). Vocabulary is clear and jargon-free. The two quotations are apt, although several shorter quotations might have given the reader a better sense of the novel. Page attributions are adequate (he might have employed footnotes). Unity in the review results from the writer's consistent consideration of the themes of invisibility and bitterness. Topic sentences are not generally strong; however, each paragraph has unity of idea, without irrelevant information.

UNIT ELEVEN
# ANALYZING WRITING STYLES

### ELEMENTS OF GOOD WRITING
### Audience, Coherence, Diction, Sources

In this unit, students apply the methods of analysis to a comparison of different writing styles. They will seek to determine the effect of audience on style and to document the various techniques that a writer uses to create a certain style.

***Discussion.*** To begin the unit, review the concept of *audience*. Explain how a writer directs a work at those who will probably read it. You can make this point effectively through the use of advertisements. Hold up a full-page magazine ad or refer to a current television commercial. Ask the class if they can tell from the ad what sort of people the advertisers are aiming at. Then examine the *diction* of the advertisement—why did the advertisers use the words they did? Ask the class to work out an ad for the same product (for example, a luxury car or a low-priced beer), using a different kind or level of diction. If the ad makes a snob appeal, students might rewrite it in slang; if it appeals to the average worker, they should make the language highbrow. Then assess the effect of the ad. To whom does it now appeal? If the ad or commercial were run this way, what would happen to the product's sales? Why?

Many magazines, like advertisements, appeal to a specific audience. You can demonstrate this by reading to the class a selection from a hobby magazine. Only those who are familiar with the jargon of the hobby (such as skiing, sewing, radio) will fully and easily understand the selection. Newspapers, too, strive to appeal to certain types of people, as you can demonstrate by comparing a tabloid with a conservative daily newspaper.

The characteristics, such as diction or word choice, tone, syntax or sentence construction, paragraph length, and use of metaphor and image, which distinguish the writing are called its *style*.

As a way of demonstrating some of the possible elements of style, and the differences between styles, have students imitate the styles of two writers. Reproduce the following paragraphs:

A  *The hotel was large, and the people kind, and all the inmates of the cart were taken in and placed on various couches. The young ensign was conveyed upstairs to Osborne's quarters. Amelia and the Major's wife had rushed down to him, when the latter had recognized him from the balcony. You may fancy the feelings of these women when they were told that the day was over, and both their husbands were safe; in what mute rapture Amelia fell on her good friend's neck, and embraced her; in what a grateful passion of prayer she fell on her knees, and thanked the Power which had saved her husband.*[26]
—W. M. THACKERAY, *VANITY FAIR*

B  *Everything was building up, closing in on me. I was trapped in so many cross turns. West Indian Archie gunning for me. The Italians who thought I'd stuck up their crap game after me. The scared kid hustler I'd hit. The cops.*[27]
—*THE AUTOBIOGRAPHY OF MALCOLM X*

Ask students to take notes on the styles of the two excerpts. Then discuss the characteristics of each and the differences between them. The discussion should include the effects of the styles as well. For example, Thackeray's use of the third person is appropriate to the description of a large and active scene, and it is necessary in order for the writer to show several physical points of view in the same passage. Malcolm X's use of first person conveys immediacy as well as the mental state of the speaker. The diction of the two pieces is appropriate to the time they were written (Thackeray: 1840s; Malcolm X: 1960s), to the reading audience, and to the impressions the authors need to convey (sentimental formality in Thackeray, desperation in Malcolm X). The sentence structure in Thackeray is ornate, well suited to the depiction of a crowded and complex scene. The raw emotion in the second paragraph, on the other hand, is effectively conveyed through short sentences, and even fragments, that grow more abrupt as the panic increases. Other stylistic points for consideration are tense (past/present), degree of detail, grammatical structure, and point of view.

These two widely different paragraphs show how different styles are appropriate to different subject matter and different audiences. Each is successful.

**Preliminary Writing.**  Students are to choose an event from the news—a short account, like that of a fire or automobile accident or sports event, works better than a long one—and rewrite it in two ways. First they should write it in the style of Thackeray's passage, preserving the elements of style that they identified in class. Then they should write it in the style of Malcolm X's excerpt, preserving the elements of his style.

**Discussion.** Have students exchange papers and read aloud either of the two paragraphs. Ask students to define the style of the piece as they hear it. Fill the board with the words they use, such as *tone, descriptive, colloquial, long sentences,* and so forth. Then categorize the terms under headings: Diction, Sentence Structure, Tone, Detail, Person, Tense, Imagery and Metaphor, and Paragraph Length. Not all of these headings may be appropriate, and you may find others. The important thing is that students learn to analyze categorically. Also they should have words ready to use for the writing assignment that follows.

**Writing.** Having seen from the preceding activity how different styles can be, students are to find two examples of different styles for analytical comparison. The examples may be excerpts from longer works. In most cases they should be one paragraph in length, although if a student chooses an excerpt from a medium, like the newspaper, that employs very short paragraphs, the excerpt will probably run to three or so paragraphs. A good place to look for material is in special interest periodicals (*Popular Mechanics, Silver Screen*). Mass circulation tabloid newspapers also have a distinctive style. Or two novels might be compared. Poetry is off-limits because the differences are likely to be either too subtle or too dramatic and because some stylistic devices are uncommon in prose.

The excerpts must be part of the papers so that a reader can see the sources. This means that if students cannot use the original or a photocopy, they must accurately copy it.

It is important that students identify their sources completely and accurately. Be sure they have this information before they begin to write the paper. The form of the citation is important, too. They must use the form you specify. The form may be from a handbook or from Unit Twelve (page 123). The paper requires a footnote for each of the two excerpts and, at the end, a bibliographical entry for each, as well.

Coherence in this sort of paper depends on the use of transitions. Comparisons of the two examples must move smoothly from one example to another. Conscious work on transitions is essential.

Good papers will go beyond mere comparisons to establish the appropriateness of the two styles. Students should explain not only *what* the characteristics of each style are but also *why* that style is appropriate.

The papers should be three to four pages long, including a page for the two excerpts. Footnotes should appear at the bottom of the page of excerpts, numbered [1] and [2]. The bibliography may be added to the last page (because this is a short paper) or appended as a separate page.

## Marking Guidelines

❖ *Audience.* Does the paper confront the issue of what audiences the two excerpts are intended for? Is it clear how the excerpts suit their styles to those audiences?

❖ *Coherence.* Are there smooth, clear transitions between the parts of the paper that discuss each of the two excerpts? Are details of the analysis arranged in a logical order?

❖ *Diction.* Has the writer included sufficient and apt examples of the diction that characterizes the two excerpts?

❖ *Sources.* Are the footnotes and bibliography accurate, complete, and formally correct?

## Sample Analysis *(excerpts are omitted)*

> The authors who wrote **The Official Preppy Handbook**, *a satirical view of preppy life, and the authors who wrote the Eddie Bauer catalog, a collection of clothes for the outdoorsman, chose drastically different styles of writing to convey their messages to the readers. Specifically, their diction, organization of details for description and narration, and sentence structure differ.*
>
> The authors of **The Preppy Handbook** *intermingled formal and informal diction to emphasize the absurdity of the subject matter. An example of this is found in the topic sentence where the colloquialisms, "hang-ups" and "go out," contrast with formal diction, "integrity," "honesty," and "lively behavioral antics." In their illustrations of various evil deeds leading to expulsion, they employ euphemistic verbs having favorable connotations of conscientiousness and diligence paired with mischievous direct objects. "Practice with your 7 iron in front of the rose window of the school chapel." "Organize a nude marathon during the board of trustees' annual meeting." "Show your chemistry teacher the highly combustible nature of nitroglycerin by blowing the squash courts just before he's due to play a match." This adds humor to the paragraph.*

The author of the Eddie Bauer catalog chose words having forceful positive connotations, for his aim was to tantalize readers to purchase a ski vest. Even the words in the vest's name, "Pro," "elite," and "new," are appealing. Adjectives describing the vest's stylish and practical features accentuate them in an attempt to entice readers to purchase a vest. These words include, "Maximum comfort," "smart-looking," "feature," and "handy inside pocket."

The paragraph from The Preppy Handbook was written to describe the process of attempting to be expelled. To inform the reader of methods of leaving with style, the author compiled a list of instructions explaining the procedure.

The writer of the advertisement from the Eddie Bauer catalog chose to define a Pro Elite ski vest as this method of paragraph development. He began by establishing the class to which the garment belonged, namely vests designed for style and maximum comfort. Next, he differentiated it from other outdoor garments. "They give lightweight warmth without the restrictions of sleeves and bulky fabrics." "The longer length warms the small of your back...."

Through variations on the simple sentence, the two authors convey dissimilar messages. The entire Eddie Bauer advertisement is composed of favorably descriptive simple sentences. This was a successful attempt to enhance the product's appeal without confusing the reader with complicated sentences. "Bauer goose down is quilted between a blend of nylon, polyester, and cotton and a sleek nylon lining." "Vests also feature zippered slash pockets and handy inside pocket for goggles."

Unlike the author of the Eddie Bauer catalog, the authors of The Preppy Handbook used command sentences to convey instructions. This was achieved by deleting the subject and beginning the sentence with a verb. "Fill your dorm room with so many Budweiser cans that the faculty room inspector can't get in the door." "Permit the school post office worker to deliver the contraband from Jamaica addressed to your box." "Borrow the brand-new Sony Trinitron...." "Practice with your 7 iron...." "Organize a nude marathon...." "Show your chemistry teacher the highly combustible nature of nitroglycerin...."

—LYNN ELLNER

**Comments.** Although the writer does not state what audience the two excerpts are intended for, she does indicate, particularly in the case of the Bauer catalog, how the author appeals to the given audience. The formal block structure for the comparison, with the writer devoting a paragraph to one excerpt and then a paragraph to another, does not require many transitional phrases; yet the paper would be stronger if there were clear transitions between some of the paragraphs (like the transition to the last paragraph). The writer has included plenty of examples of diction and sentence structure to illustrate her generalizations.

Footnotes and bibliography, not included here, are exemplified in Unit Twelve.

UNIT TWELVE
# ARGUING A POSITION

### ELEMENTS OF GOOD WRITING
### Development, Sources, Unity

In this unit, which calls for a researched argumentative paper, process is at least as important as product. The final writing is not so long (four to five pages), but its preparation should be a careful undertaking of several steps. In order to emphasize that students should take pains with each step of the process, give grades for each part: choice and use of sources, note cards, outline, rough draft, and final draft. These activities give you a chance to teach note-taking skills and to show students how to avoid plagiarism by documenting their sources.

*Discussion.* Begin by warming up the class for argumentative topics. Mention some controversial subjects and ask the students what they think. To start with, use issues on which they can express an opinion without doing research. You might, for example, say, "I read recently that on any given weekend night in this country, one out of every ten drivers on the road is drunk. Drunk drivers cause more accidents each year than they did in the previous year. Maybe the bars and liquor stores should be closed at 6:00 P.M. every Friday and Saturday. What do you think of that?"

Other topics on which students can immediately and actively take sides come from such things as school politics ("The Student Council should monitor study halls") and sports ("The National League should adopt the designated hitter rule"; "Girls should be allowed to play on the boys' basketball team").

Next raise some more complex, less familiar issues. The best topics for this purpose are those about which students know something, but only a little. Present some information, but not too much, to support your conclusion—long presentations can be boring. Furthermore, the desirable student response is "I can't tell," or "It depends," or "We need to know more before we can decide." The point is for students to recognize that research is necessary. Later, in doing that research, they will have to accommodate information and arguments counter to their own positions. Developing an argumentative topic requires acknowledgement of the other side as well as a convincing presentation of one's own point of view.

Examples of more complex topics:

> Even though the military budget of the United States is increasing, our defenses against nuclear attack are growing more and more inadequate as other nations unveil more and more sophisticated weapons. The one U.S. deterrent that is virtually unassailable is the MX missile. We must immediately divert funds from other defense projects to develop and deploy the MX missile.

> A network of canals, combined with speculative development projects, is gradually draining away the Everglades in Florida. Many species of wildlife, like alligators and egrets, are threatened with extinction. In order not to lose this unique swamp environment, we must halt development and fill in most of the canals.

For other complex issues you could develop, look to standard debate topics, such as abortion, euthanasia, wage and price controls, tariffs on imports, and abolition of the electoral college. If some students are quick to take sides, ask questions like these: "Why?" "What are your reasons?" "Are there other important arguments on that side?" As they consider these issues, students come to see that they cannot make a strong case either for or against these positions without the use of sources to inform and support them.

An argumentative topic that requires research is the starting point for the writing assignment. Spend some class time brainstorming for such topics.

After brainstorming, give students a day to choose their individual argumentative topics. Although students should select topics similar in complexity to those on the list produced in class, they should try to find original topics that interest them. Because it is likely that students will be sharing the facilities of one or two libraries, duplication of topics can lead to confusion and unhealthy competition for sources.

**Prewriting.** As students disclose and briefly explain their topics in class, encourage them to narrow or focus those topics so that they are appropriate for a paper of four to five pages. For example, a paper will be overly general and lacking in unity if a student tries to develop such a thesis as "The Vietnam War was unproductive" or "Wilderness laws are necessary to protect the ecology." On the other hand, if the student can argue that the Vietnam War caused the United States to lose prestige with Japan, or that a wilderness law can help to save the grizzly bear in Alaska's Brooks Range, unity is more likely, and the writer can make more efficient use of source material.

***Preliminary Writing.***  The point of this activity is to ensure that students know how to take accurate notes, complete with bibliographical information, from their sources. Choose a book to which the whole class has access. Ideal for this activity is a collection of short essays, but in fact almost anything other than a poetry anthology will do.

Choose a selection of two or three pages that students are to read and take notes from. They should use 3 × 5 index cards for notes. Students should indicate with quotation marks actual quotations from sources; paraphrases and summaries should not be enclosed in quotation marks. Be sure to remind the class, however, that use of another's ideas, as in paraphrasing or summarizing, requires footnoting just as direct quotation does. Not to acknowledge the source is to plagiarize.

Invent a topic (it need not be argumentative) for which the selection is appropriate as a source so students have a clear direction for their note taking. They are not to abstract the entire selection—only those portions that apply to the topic.

Notes should occupy the fronts of the cards; on the backs should be identification of sources. The back of the first card should supply full bibliographical information: author, title of selection, title of book, editor (where applicable), place of publication, publisher, date of publication, and page number. Do not yet prescribe a specific form, but tell students to be sure to include all of this information. Subsequent cards on the same book need mention only author and page.

***Discussion.***   Students should exchange cards and check for:
- ◇ accurate transcription of quotations
- ◇ useful summaries of key ideas
- ◇ complete bibliographical information

Then have students return the cards. Now explain the proper form for both footnotes and bibliography.

You may wish to use a more inclusive reference, like the *MLA Handbook* (Modern Language Association, 1977), or a handbook already in use in school to specify form; however, here are sample entries that will suffice for most short research papers.

### FOOTNOTES

Book by one author:

[1] William Graham Sumner, *Folkways* (New York: Mentor, 1960), p. 93.

Book by two or more authors:

[2] Idelle Sullens, Edith Karas, and Raymond Fabrizio, *The Inquiring Reader* (Boston: Heath, 1967), p. 151.

Article or essay in a book:

[3] Dorothy Parker, "The Standard of Living," in *50 Great Short Stories,* ed. Milton Crane (New York: Bantam, 1971), pp. 25-27.

Encyclopedia:

[4] "Bella Coola," *New Century Cyclopedia of Names,* Vol. 1, 1954, p. 437.

Magazine article:

[5] John N. Cole, "The Vanishing Tuna," *Atlantic,* December 1976, p. 49.

Newspaper article:

[6] "Low-Power TV Project Is Delayed," *New York Times,* 19 January 1981, p. D1.

Interview:

[7] Interview with Roland Glover, 18 December 1980, DeLand, Illinois.

Because other possibilities exist, it is best to have another, more complete, reference list available. If you give the list above to students, draw their attention to the magazine and newspaper entries. Sometimes in a magazine the author is not supplied, and in that case the entry begins with the title of the article.

Subsequent references to a footnoted source need mention only the author's name and page number (for example, [8]Cole, p. 50). However, if the writer uses more than one work by the same author, the footnote should also include the title of the book or article.

A bibliography is appended to a paper. Bibliographical entries look like footnotes except that the list is alphabetical, by author; the author's name is written last name first; periods separate parts of the entry; publication data is not enclosed in parentheses; and page numbers are given only for an article in a magazine or newspaper or a selection from an anthology.

### BIBLIOGRAPHY

"Bella Coola." *New Century Cyclopedia of Names*, Vol. 1, 1954.

Cole, John N. "The Vanishing Tuna." *Atlantic.* December 1976, pp. 48-54.

Glover, Roland. Interview. 18 December 1980, DeLand, Illinois.

"Low-Power TV Project Is Delayed." *New York Times.* 19 January 1981, p. D1.

Parker, Dorothy, "The Standard of Living." In *50 Great Short Stories.* Edited by Milton Crane. New York: Bantam, 1971.

Sullens, Idelle, Edith Karas, and Raymond Fabrizio. *The Inquiring Reader.* Boston: Heath, 1967.

Sumner, William Graham. *Folkways.* New York: Mentor, 1960.

Now students should commence their research. If possible, work closely with school or public librarians. Perhaps they can give the class a library tour and can help students to locate sources. In any case, be sure to let the librarians know that your class is coming.

**Preliminary Writing.** Once the research is well underway, ask students for a thesis statement. One paragraph in length, this statement should establish the unity of the paper by stating the major contention. A good thesis statement will also suggest how the paper's development will proceed by mentioning the key ideas that the writer will use to convince the audience of the assertion in the thesis.

**Prewriting.** As research is proceeding, ask for an outline of the paper. You may wish to specify a particular form for the outline. In any case, it should begin with the thesis statement, and it should include every idea that the writer plans to develop. It should also refer to at least four quotations or paraphrases from the writer's sources. To ensure unity in the paper, each item in the outline must be clearly relevant to the thesis at the beginning.

**Writing.** The paper is to be four to five pages in length, exclusive of the bibliography. Students must incorporate at least *four quotations* from sources; these must be footnoted and the sources must be listed in the bibliography. Additional quotations, as well as paraphrases and summaries, require footnote and bibliography entries also. All source acknowledgements must be complete and accurate, according to the prescribed form. Furthermore, students must use at least *three different sources*, and these must include at least two different types (types include encyclopedias, periodicals, newspapers, books).

A rough draft must precede the final paper. Use this draft to check the development of the paper. The draft must contain enough clearly stated evidence to make a convincing case for the assertion of the thesis statement. Since no argument is wholly one-sided, a well-developed paper must acknowledge, though briefly, the key arguments on the other side of the question. Perhaps those arguments can serve as a starting point for the paper, as the writer states the objections to the course of action he or she is proposing and then presents the far more weighty advantages of his or her own position. The rough draft should end with an emphatic conclusion.

The rough draft also provides an opportunity to ascertain that students' sources are introduced smoothly into the text and are properly acknowledged. Phrases such as "In an article in the *Atlantic*, John Cole claims, ' . . . '" and "According to the naturalist John Muir, ' . . . '" help the reader along; a footnote is necessary, too.

After you have examined and commented on the rough drafts, students should carefully edit them before they prepare the final copy. Allow two days for this, one a workshop day in class.

The final version of the research argument should be neat, clean, free of error—and persuasive.

### Marking Guidelines

◆ *Development.* Has the writer used enough evidence to convince the audience? Within the length guidelines, is the paper thorough? Has the writer acknowledged contrary arguments and effectively overcome them?

❖ *Sources.* Has the writer used at least four quotations, at least three different sources, and at least two types of sources? Is each quotation, paraphrase, and summary introduced with a transitional phrase within the text? Is each reference accurately footnoted? Do footnotes and bibliography follow the prescribed form?

❖ *Unity.* Does the paper begin with a clear thesis statement that includes the important ideas in the paper? Do all of the parts of the argument bear on the thesis?

## Sample Paper

*The Vietnam War began in 1957 when the Communist North Vietnamese forces attacked the government in South Vietnam. The Communists wanted to unite Vietnam under one rule in order to stop the South Vietnamese government from acting as a "puppet" of the United States. Starting as guerilla and terrorists fights, the war grew to threaten world peace. There was much controversy over the fact that the U.S. economically aided the South Vietnamese army and began to send U.S. troops into a civil war. The U.S. had fully entered the war by 1967 because President Johnson wanted to prevent the spread of communism.[1] The war ended in 1973 and it was the duration that caused tremendous casualties. Because the Vietnamese war was in a stalemate and both countries showed an eagerness to end the war in 1968, the United States should have withdrawn from the war at this time and begun peace talks instead of prolonging the disaster.*

*First, during the war neither the American forces nor the North Vietnamese forces were making progress. For example, there were no decisive victories on either side.[2] The Tet Offensive, a large scale of North Vietnamese attacks in South Vietnam, displayed the futility of all the battles during the war. The Communists caused heavy destruction and death in Hue and Saigon when they launched the Tet Offensive in February of 1968. In the longest battle of the Vietnam War, the Communist forces attacked the U.S. Marine base located in the city of Khe Sanh in 1968. The North Vietnamese troops were forced to withdraw after a 77-day siege because their army was slowly being destroyed.[3] Then, in mid 1968 the U.S. Marines and some other U.S. security troops withdrew from this area because of a psychological weakening caused by the North Vietnamese attacks.[4] U.S. citizens viewed the battles as defeats although the American Commander claimed victory.[5]*

*In addition, the casualties of both the American and Vietnamese armies were extremely high. In this war more U.S. men were killed than in any other war. During the war, 57,000 U.S. troops died* which included 46,600 in combat. The United States forces had a total of 213,514 casualties, and another 150,375 people were wounded but didn't require hospital care.[6] Also, many Americans who served in the war have permanent severe psychological problems today. South Vietnamese forces suffered about 254,300 troop deaths. North Vietnamese and Viet Cong troop deaths totalled about 1,027,000.[7] The Vietnamese also had experienced massive destruction in vast areas of their land.

Second, in 1968 the United States and North Vietnam both made statements indicating a readiness for negotiation, but failed to actually negotiate. For example, President Johnson declared on September 29, 1967, that he would "stop all bombing if this action would lead to productive discussions."[8] Two views, both in favor of ending the war, existed in the United States about what the administration should do about the war. A group of Americans advocated a saturation bombing of Haiphong, Hanoi, and the Red River Dikes in North Vietnam. Many other Americans, in contrast, believed that the United States should totally withdraw from the war.[9] Furthermore, Secretary General Thant said that if the United States stopped bombing Vietnam, "it could assume that North Vietnam would deal in good faith with the issue of ground fighting."[10] North Vietnamese Foreign Minister Trinh expressed his desire for the aggressive war to terminate when he suggested that the United States withdraw forces from Vietnam.[11] The Vietnamese people didn't care how the war, which had caused them so much suffering, came to an end as long as it did stop.

Finally, rather than carrying the war on for five more years, the United States should have both withdrawn forces and begun negotiations in 1968 when the two factors of a stalemate in the war and a readiness of the countries to end the war occurred. For example, Senator Robert F. Kennedy attacked the Johnson administration by saying, "The history among nations does not record any such lengthy and consistent chronicle of error as that brought about by the U.S. in Vietnam."[12]

---

[1] "Vietnam War," The World Book Encyclopedia, Vol. 20, p. 293.
[2] Bernard B. Fall, "Our Options in Vietnam," Reporter, March 1964, p. 17.
[3] Vietnam War," p. 292h.
[4] Peter Braestrup, Big Story (Denver: Freedom House, 1977), Vol. 1, p. 557.
[5] "Chronology of Events in Conflicts in Asia," The New York Times, 19 February 1979, sec. 1, p. 17.

[6] *"Casualties in Principal Wars of the U.S.," The World Almanac, 1981, p. 744.*
[7] *"Vietnam War," p. 292h.*
[8] *"Thant Urges U.S. Assume Hanoi Good Faith in Talks," The New York Times, 25 January 1968, sec. 1, p. 1.*
[9] *"The War," Time Magazine, March 1, 1968, pp. 1-2.*
[10] *"Thant Urges U.S. Assume Hanoi Good Faith in Talks," The New York Times, 25 January 1968, sec. 1, p. 1.*
[11] *"Hanoi Indicates It Is Still Ready to Discuss Peace," The New York Times, 9 January 1968, sec. 1, p. 1.*
[12] *Tom Wicker, "Kennedy Asserts U.S. Cannot Win," The New York Times, 9 January 1968, sec. 1, p. 1.*

## Bibliography

Braestrup, Peter. Big Story. Denver: Freedom House, 1977.

"Cambodian Decision: Why President Acted." The New York Times, 30 June 1970, sec. 1, p. 1.

"Casualties in Principal Wars of the U.S." The World Almanac. 1981.

"Chronology of Events in Conflicts in Asia." The New York Times, 19 February 1979, sec. 1, p. 17.

Fall, Bernard B. "Our Options in Vietnam." Reporter, March 1964, p. 17.

Fall, Bernard B. Vietnam Witness. New York: Frederick A. Praeger, 1966.

"Hanoi Indicates It Is Still Ready to Discuss Peace." The New York Times, 9 January 1968, sec. 1, p. 1.

"Last Combat Unit Out of Cambodia." The New York Times, 30 June 1970, sec. 1, p. 1.

"No Bucks for the Bang." Newsweek, 17 March 1973, pp. 43-44.

"Thant Urges U.S. Assume Hanoi Good Faith in Talks." The New York Times, 25 January 1968, sec. 1, p. 1.

"The War." Time Magazine, 1 March 1968, pp. 1-2.

"Vietnam War." The World Book Encyclopedia. 1980.

Wicker, Tom. "Kennedy Asserts U.S. Cannot Win." The New York Times, 9 January 1968, sec. 1, p. 1.

—KENNETH RADER

**Comments.** The writer has made a very broad topic (the Vietnam War) into a narrower argument (the United States should have pulled out of Vietnam in 1968). Still, his sources provide so much material that development is broad and necessarily incomplete. However, the Tet Offensive (paragraph two) is a good choice for a developed example both because it is typical of the frustration of the war and because it occurred in 1968. The writer uses sources well, drawing helpful statistics from them, and gracefully introduces quotations in his text. The quotation with which he closes is appropriate and well handled. Footnotes and bibliography are correct. Unity in the paper is directed by a thesis statement placed emphatically at the end of the first paragraph. In the third paragraph, unity suffers because the writer does not directly connect the casualty figures to the "1968" part of his thesis. But an opening transition in the next paragraph reasserts the paper's unity.

## NOTES

1 Jacques Barzun, "The State of Writing Today" (Unpublished speech given at the University of Texas at Arlington, 3 March 1977).

2 Jeb Stuart Magruder, *An American Life* (New York: Atheneum, 1974), p. 228.

3 James Reston, *The Artillery of the Press* (New York: Harper & Row, 1966), p. 47.

4 Linda Goodman, *Linda Goodman's Sun Signs* (New York: Taplinger Publishing Co., 1968), p. 189.

5 E.B. White, "Questionnaire," in *One Man's Meat* (New York: Harper & Row, 1944), p. 296.

6 John Foster Dulles, quoted by Bertrand Russell in a letter to the editor of *Harper's Magazine*, June 1963.

7 Sir Winston Churchill, *The Second World War* (New York: Time, Inc., 1959), p. 294.

8 E.B. White, "Once More to the Lake," in *One Man's Meat* (New York: Harper & Row, 1944), p. 248.

9 Marya Mannes, *But Will It Sell?* (Philadelphia: J.B. Lippincott Co., 1961), p. 48.

10 Eric Severeid, *This Is Eric Severeid* (New York: McGraw-Hill, 1964), p. 27.

11 John F. Kennedy, *To Turn the Tide* (New York: Harper & Row, 1962), p. 31.

12 Anne Sinclair Mehdevi, *Persia Revisited* (New York: Alfred Knopf, 1965), p. 132.

13   E.B. White, "Sootfall and Fallout," in *Essays of E.B. White* (New York: Harper & Row, 1977), p. 95.

14   Rumer Godden, *Gypsy, Gypsy* (New York: Viking, 1940), p. 90.

15   Elie Wiesel, *One Generation After* (New York: Random House, 1970), p. 169.

16   Mary McCarthy, *Birds of America* (New York: Harcourt Brace Jovanovich, 1965), p. 169.

17   A. Scott Berg, *Max Perkins: Editor of Genius* (New York: E.P. Dutton, 1978), p. 24.

18   Joan Didion, *The White Album* (New York: Simon & Schuster, 1979), p. 221.

19   John Philip Baumgardt, *How to Prune Almost Anything* (New York: William Morrow, 1968), p. 7.

20   J. Bronowski, *The Ascent of Man* (Boston: Little, Brown, 1973), p. 155.

21   Henry Kissinger, *White House Years* (Boston: Little, Brown, 1978), p. 150.

22   John Ruskin, *The Stones of Venice* (Boston: D. Estes & Co., n.d.), v. 1, p. 207.

23   Amelia Earhart, *Last Flight* (New York: Harcourt, Brace and Co., 1937), p. 82.

24   Charles Dickens, *Bleak House* (New York: Harper & Bros., n.d.), p. 11.

25   Edgar Allen Poe, "The Fall of the House of Usher," in *The Fall of the House of Usher and Other Tales* (New York: New American Library, 1960), p. 113.

26   William Makepeace Thackeray, *Vanity Fair* (New York: Signet, 1962), p. 376.

27   Malcolm X, *The Autobiography of Malcolm X* (New York: Grove Press, 1965), p. 132.

**About the Author**

Paul Kalkstein has been an instructor in English since 1965, first at the Choate School in Wallingford, Connecticut, and since 1970 at the Phillips Academy in Andover, Massachusetts. He is a former member of the Commission on Writing of the Council for Basic Education and is an Associate on the National Humanities Faculty. He is co-author of *English Competence Handbook*. A graduate of the Phillips Academy and Princeton University, he holds a Master's degree from Yale University. He lives with his wife and three children in Andover, Massachusetts.

## *Also from Fearon Teacher Aids...*

### *Creative Escapes: Adventures in Writing for Grades 7–12*
by Barbara Christian
Supplement your basic language arts curriculum with these highly motivating exercises in grammar and creative writing. A hands-on idea book, **Creative Escapes** offers you more than 30 classroom-tested composition activities. Following a brief introduction, each activity includes lists of objectives and required materials; a suggested teaching sequence; writing samples, topic ideas, and other teaching aids; and teaching notes. Most activities feature options and variations for gifted students. You'll find the book's appeal to the interests and concerns of today's adolescent just what you need to motivate students at all levels. 128 pages; 6" x 9"; illustrated; paperbound; 1631–X.

### *You Are the Editor*
by Eric Johnson
This book is an exciting new approach to improving the writing of students in fifth grade through high school. Its carefully designed lessons teach students to be editors; to use the symbols professional editors use; to correct the spelling and punctuation errors editors correct; and to evaluate style, tone, and organization the way editors do. But learning to edit is not an end in itself. The editing that students do on the lesson pages is editing they will continue to do on their own papers, improving the quality of their written work and saving you, the teacher, countless hours of correcting papers. Available in two versions. MAKEMASTER® Blackline Masters: 144 pages; 8½" x 11"; perforated; three-hole drilled; paperbound; 7696–7. Consumable workbook: 64 pages; 8½" x 11"; paperbound; 7697–5. Accompanying teacher's guide: 7698–3.